SECOND EDITION

THE CHICANO LABYRINTH OF SOLITUDE
A STUDY IN THE MAKING OF THE CHICANO MIND AND CHARACTER

E.C. OROZCO

Kendall Hunt
publishing company

publishing company

www.kendallhunt.com
Send all inquiries to:
4050 Westmark Drive
Dubuque, IA 52004-1840

Printed in the United States of America
10 9 8 7 6 5 4 3

DEDICATED TO

RODOLFO "CORKY" GONZALES

AN ODE TO A MACHIOTL

There was once a man named Corky Gonzales,
professional boxing was his game,
inspired, this oracle of a man wrote a poema,
with piercing words that earned him fame,

His enduring spiritual poema, **I am Joaquin★**,
was more than just a personal fleeting chant,
it narrated the lamentable struggle of a people,
in pain,

Chicanos owe much to this stout machiotl,
whose words stirred the hearts of a people,
and ignited a Chicano cultural renaissance,
in Aztlan.

The waning bond of carnalismo was heartened,
to liberate those astray in a labyrinth of solitude,
and emerged as the unwavering psychic force,
to effect a spiritual catharsis of La Raza.

c/s

E. C. Orozco

★The poema in film of **I am Joaquin** was directed and narrated
by Luis Valdez in 1969.

Contents

Introduction

*I*n no other region in the world will a casual observer find so many Anglo-Saxon-like English-speaking "Mexicans" as in the southwestern United States. Easterners who visit or resettle in the Southwest are often mildly surprised to encounter this American type in such vast numbers. But like the "native" Caucasian stock of the region, many of the more recent arrivals gradually acquire the same antagonistic and contemptuous sentiments toward the brown, Spanish-speaking Americans. Americans they may be, but "Mexicans" and second-class citizens they remain in the Anglo ethos and general mental framework.

Mexican nationals, Europeans, Asians, and South American immigrants are similarly impressed by the large brown American and Mexican population resident in the cities of Los Angeles, San Antonio, and Albuquerque. However, many Mexicans and South Americans are repulsed by the weak and self-effacing brown American character. Moreover, since many South American immigrants import a distinctive class consciousness, they view working-class Mexican Americans as social inferiors. Nonetheless, Spanish-speaking non-citizens are soon motivated to distance themselves from resident brown Americans.

Because, in all candor, it is laborious for anyone, including for most Latinos, to truly comprehend, and consequently to learn to respect the brown American because of the latter's profound and endless struggle with his self-identity. But, then, that is the labyrinth of solitude and confusion they are cast into by American society. Naturally, it is interesting to note how upon entering the region many Mexican nationals and South Americans identify with Mexican Americans due to an imagined cultural and racial affinity. The attraction and attachment often ends abruptly when they learn that many native-born Mexican Americans are anti-Hispano-Mexican brown-skinned Anglos and not Latinos. In the process these foreigners also discover that many Mexican Americans possess an acute inferiority complex, in concert with a strange and unrealistic aspiration to want to be white.

Conversely, many brown-aspiring Anglo natives do not particularly appreciate the endless flow of Spanish-speaking foreigners. Feelings of inferiority surface because it draws attention to their non-white physical appearance in the daily white American setting. It is hardly a secret to those who live and work among Mexican Americans that many suffer from a lack of self-esteem and pride in their indigenous race and Mexican heritage.

Most casual observers, including most foreigners, are unaware of the historical Mexican-Anglo cultural clash and struggle for power in the Southwest. While some may be aware of the 1848 Treaty of Guadalupe Hidalgo which terminated open hostilities between Mexico and the United States, most are totally ignorant of the negative psychological processing and socialization brown Americans experience in the public schools and in American society generally.

Frankly, what foreigner would know that the national history, ethos, and institutions of the United States advance an anti-Hispano-Mexican drift of thought, a legacy that infers brown Americans lost the natural right of self-determination and cultural uniqueness? Moreover, what white American or brown American, reared outside the barrio fringes of the Chicano experience, would accept the suggestion that the identity and linguistic problems, and most of the social evils in the brown American community, are natural by-products of the group's counter-cultural resistance to the dominant society's pernicious efforts to suppress and eradicate the brown American's Hispano-Mexican heritage? Or, that brown Americans are denied the natural right to exist as equals in the American experience?

Mexican American behavior, and the community's negative self-images, solitude, and inferiority complex is symptomatic of much more than any natural or self-imposed lack of pride of heritage witnessed by "outsiders" and new arrivals to Aztlan (United States Southwest). Coarsely ignorant and generally insensitive to the historical sequences and anti-Mexican social guides, which markedly intended that Mexicans should remain culturally submissive and inferior, the outsider is guided to believe brown Americans do not assume the onus of responsibility for success in "America." Success, American propagandists assure us, rests entirely with the individual regardless of obstacles.

The American doctrine that all an individual requires is faith, will, and heart is swallowed hook, line, and sinker by the socially insensitive and ignorant who come under its pervasive influence and material sway. Ignored or overlooked are the historical stages of subordination; the first stage being the cultural suppression of the Mexicans, their physical isolation, and denial of equal access to opportunity and wealth. This, in concert with the false conviction that a "Mexican" must separate himself from his culture and race to become American, although he may be American-born. The second stage now current is psychological apartheid.

Moreover, the rationale and blueprint for material success slights the natural right "to be" tenet of all Americans guaranteed by the Constitution. The monoculturalism of "false" Americanism with its supremacist "melting pot" credo has, in effect, corrupted the original tenets of American liberty. Thus, cultures and languages that theoretically hinder progressive individual material success in Anglo-American society must recede before the "American." The false credo that only the Americanized can achieve material success is advanced and reinforced by the glorification of the one race and culture over the other. American assimilation and subordination of the will to that end is the socially directed ultimate goal. Mexican Americans and Chicanos, therefore, are expected to commit ethnocide for their own material good.

Mexican precedence in the Southwest notwithstanding, many Mexican Americans have endorsed the "melting pot" creed of monoracial and monocultural "false" Americanism propagated by white American supremacism. Issues of race, culture, religion, and self-identity are made life-long problems for brown Americans. More than one hundred years of social exclusion, racism, and cruel isolation has demonstrated to all persons who care that these problems cannot be resolved simply by changing lifestyles and one's name. The culture of La Raza is indigenous to the Southwest. It predated the present dominant English-speaking society. Moreover, due to the group's physical and spiritual precedence in the region, and its proximity to Mexico and the country's Anglophile, it will doubtless keep the brown American distinctly and uniquely Chicano.

This study focuses on the Southwest's unique anti-Hispano Mexican American environment in which Americans of all races and ethnic backgrounds are presently nurtured. Although persons of Mexican descent can be found in every state of the union, the great majority reside in the United States Southwest. In simple terms they are generally southwestern Americans. This study also concentrates on the public schools' major monopolized cultural countering role in the making of the Chicano mind and character.

The American public school influence on Mexican Americans is a relatively new national experience. Lamentably, close review and examination of the evidence points to the schools as the major obstacle to the development of self-esteem, brown American success, and first-class citizenship. And, in effect, it is the schools that reshape many Chicanos into what some brown American scholars refer to as non-colonized non-Chicanos. In short, the public schools effortlessly emerge as the most insensitive institutional culprit of all American agencies that determine Chicano and Mexican American thought and behavior.

In review, becoming a non-colonized non-Chicano is not the worst possible consequence, or even the most critical issue. The insensitive and cruel process that produces the negative by-product, the marginal personality, is the overlooked key to the problem. Indeed, it is central to synthesizing at least a fringe of understanding of the origin of many of the social evils that beset the brown American community. The means or process to change, to accommodation, to eventual partial social inclusion, is psychologically harmful and adverse to the healthy development of the brown child. In truth, it is a process that promotes collective subservience, shame, and aversive conditioning to Chicanismo, Mexicanism, and to brownness.

In the past, courage, faith, and a remarkable people culture protected and sustained members of the brown community from socio-psychological assaults from without. Those cultural safeguards and defenses have been eroded and fragmented since the 1940s, invariably by the negative pervasive influence of the public school's social curriculum. The cultural marginalism animated among Mexican Americans by the schools has had a socially and psychologically negative impact in the brown American community.

American public schools pose and generate many problems and obstacles for brown children. The critical commentary made by then-Education Secretary William Bennett in 1988 of our public school products as "unacceptably low" and "poorly educated," is notably consistent with our contention regarding the schools as it relates to barrio youngsters. Mr. Bennett's candid remarks concerning the dropout rate among minorities as "perilously high" echoes our alarm regarding Chicano and other brown children.

Social scientists know that adulthood is not a stage of life during which a personality automatically or suddenly accelerates self-actualization. Persons are products of their social institutional environments. In this connection, we closely examine the country's institutionalized mechanisms and built-in reinforcing agencies aimed at sustaining the disoriented and marginal status of its colored minorities. Evidently, the purpose of institutionalized racism and social exclusion is intended to nurture and perpetuate social cues that reinforce subordinated minority behavior and thinking, even should it no longer be publicly sanctioned. The schools methodically set the mental framework and social patterns. Students simply respond to the long-established societal pattern cues learned in school.

This book focuses on one of the major causes for the present widespread social and psychological maladjustment of the brown American Spanish surnamed community: the public schools. The social pitfalls of a culture of separation, discrimination, and the social intimidation of a colored minority are also highlighted; and, the dangerous insensitivity perpetrated by the Chicano de-socialization process. The following conclusion also holds true. That is, that society's means to an end inoperative "false" American idealism is creating and nurturing explosive socio-psychological conditions in the barrios, and among Spanish-speaking immigrants and socially marginalized mobile brown Americans.

The writings of brown Spanish surnamed women in the ivory tower, as an example, are infused with leftist literary fantasies such as postcolonialism and internationalism reminiscent of universal socialist doctrine. In brief, academic intellectual notions that are irrelevant to the Chicano community which, when tested, instead of healing often result in further cultural alienation and confusion among Mexican American young people. This second edition also examines the marginalized brown American woman's socialist and American white woman's liberation influences in their disquisitions, and their references to broader sexuality issues, homosexuality, machismo, their not too subtle disdain for collective Mexicanism and Chicanismo.

The reader should not assume the author's academic deciphering of the labyrinth of marginalized brown women's behavior and theorizing represents an oppositional stance to Chicana feminism. On the contrary, most brown college students surveyed acknowledge there are positive and negative points to feminism. But, it is self-evident many brown women theorists have gone, or were reared, beyond the secure nepantla of the barrio as aspirants to a more vague individualized consciousness and space or new nepantla between Chicanismo and gabachismo; thereby, intensifying the confusion of self-identity in the brown American ivory tower.

I should like to thank my colleagues, Professors Daniel Tiberi and the late John Reib, for their suggestions and support in writing this manuscript. And, also, Professor G. E. Miranda. Nonetheless, authoritative quotations and citations were kept to a minimum and were used in those cases deemed academically indispensable. However, a study of this nature would not have been possible without the keen and penetrating questions asked by my Chicano Studies students during the past three decades. It also represents the summation of my years of teaching at the primary and secondary school levels, and nearly fifteen years of work experience with brown youth groups and gangs. Nevertheless, intensive years of study and research were imperative to synthesize the brown American socio-psychological experience into a coherent framework. That was the primary goal of this study and the author is both confident and hopeful that end was accomplished.

E.C.O., 2012

CHAPTER 1

The Formative Years:

Self-Images and Expectations

*M*ost children's formative years are critically important to their later mental development. The most permanent and profound ideas, self-images, and self-expectations are therein concretely and irreversibly impressed. Thus, with the inception of early childhood experiences the basic foundation of an individual's personality has root in this chronological span. In the varied dimensions of educational psychology this development process is axiomatic. In effect, it is a condition generally endorsed by most educators in view of the fact the cornerstones of our educational philosophy is structured on a pyramidical approach from grades K through 12.

In short, the school's finite purpose is fourfold: (1) to nurture secular humanistic values and attitudes, (2) to cultivate good citizenship, (3) to teach reading, writing, and arithmetic, and (4) to advance a White Anglo-Saxon Republican Protestant middle class social status quo milieu. The schools' nationalizing ideological program seeks to minimize communalism. But there is more. Ideologically the aim is to minimize and mitigate as much as possible the ethnic, class, religious, and socioeconomic differences among the citizenry of the land. This requires the systematic impression of an uncompromising new and distinctive secular universalizing process. The Americanization process has popularly come to be called the "melting pot."

In time, the Establishment Americanization process has evolved as the means by which to socially stratify ethnics, or colored persons, who cannot or will not relinquish their corporeate attachments, and subordinate their biological identification.[1] The program's social directives mandate cultural and racial alienation of all its potential members. American public schools' secular humanist educational philosophy is fanatically guided by that social format and principle.[2] Moreover, brown Americans are currently in the throes of this process.[3]

Children do not enter school for the first time devoid of a certain degree of cognitive development. Psychologists recognize that since birth, and perhaps before birth, a child's operational structures are functioning. Further, sensory-motor operations are at their optimum during the first two years of life and concrete thinking operations come into play during the next two through ten years. In addition, there are sub-stages of these major steps of development which we need not enter into here. The point that should be stressed is that social scientists accept the fact children enter school with some definite ideas of what and who they are.

Moreover, a child's self-identification (whether positive or negative) is indispensably critical at this chronological time since it determines to a maximum degree the reinforcement or lowering of his basic ego-strength. It is presumed by many educators that if the child stems from a home where he is appreciated and loved, invariably he will reflect emotional stability and a positive self-image; and, subsequent so-called normal behavior. Pre-school children's stability or instability, then, commonly rests on the home environment at this chronological stage of psychological growth.

---

1. Corporate is used in this study in the reference to a corporal religio-philosophical ethnic community.

2. To break down ethnic and racial differences, to individualize the human personality. To integrate into a new whole the disintegrated individuals of foreign host cultures and races. This applies to all citizens except the colored minorities.

3. The great majority of persons of Mexican descent are of indigenous American (Indian) descent. Also, the vast majority of Mexican Americans are United States born and reared citizens. Although the majority has been influenced by a barrio way of life in the United States, it is also true that the social curriculum of the schools, the media, and social interaction with white Americans has been more pronounced in the past generation than previously. The group is mostly culturally Chicano. Our attempt to incorporate Mexican immigrants and, therefore, Indo-Hispanics, and barrio raised Chicanos and non-barrio reared browns, generated the need for a common denominator—a term that encompasses the vast majority. The only common denominator is race, thus the application of the brown American. To attempt to identify this group by surname is fallacious and dishonest. A black Anglo does not, for example, become white simply because he is a fifth generation American with an English surname.

While it may be superfluous to point out that brown children are normal and like other youngsters, it is, nevertheless, necessary to point out that brown children also constitute a wide range composite of emotional stability and instability proportionate to their numbers. In view of the generally larger families, impoverished living conditions, and mythical "macho fathers" and masochistic mothers, a greater incidence of emotional instability would be expected, almost anticipated; but the available evidence demonstrates these expectations are absent. Conversely, brown children are especially well-mannered, healthy, clean, and, once they have adjusted to a school situation, well-behaved. In short, all the signs of good mental health are present in Mexican American children. Like most healthy and normal children, they are ready to begin school and, invariably, are just as enthusiastic. What the schools do to this motivation and enthusiasm is one of the tragedies and scandals of American public school education.

THE CAUSES FOR BILINGUALISM

The linguistic development of children is particularly noticeable in the first four grade levels. In a short span of four to five years a child's vocabulary expands and grows from a limited egocentric level to a more socialized degree. In comparison, it is both an interesting and instructive point of fact that Spanish surname children's language skills and vocabulary expand as normally in their social environment as among the supposedly more democratically influenced, and verbal-oriented Caucasian youngsters. Evidently brown American children are accorded sufficient opportunity to discuss, explain, and collaborate within the family circle and in the barrio.

Loyd S. Tireman found in the 1940s that New Mexico Spanish-speaking children possessed a Spanish vocabulary of some two thousand words by the time they entered kindergarten. Tireman's pioneer study, although dated, serves to illustrate the relatively well-conceptualized world of the rural pre-school, Spanish-speaking child.[4] Since Tireman's study the world of Spanish-speaking rural Chicano children has become more urban-like given the fact television has long been introduced (in both English and Spanish) even among the very poor.

---

4. Loyd S. Tireman, "Meaning and Reading," *Proceedings, Fifth Annual Conference, Southwest Council on Education of the Spanish Speaking People,* Los Angeles, California, 1951, p. 19.

Therefore, it would be remiss or faulty to conjecture that Chicano preschoolers do not amass a more pronounced and expanded vocabulary than their predecessors of the 1940s.

A functional English or Spanish vocabulary is an incidental and indispensable acquisition, particularly among urban Chicano children. Given the reality that language is a major persistent cultural influence which survives most strongly, its early and consequently psychologically permanent acquisition is irrefutable. Moreover, intimately acquired linguistic mental impulses are emotionally potent. Language, after all, is the symbolic world that binds a white Chicano with a brown or black Chicano. It is the soul or whatever symbol man may provide to describe the spiritual cord of a people.

Perhaps due to these specific reasons, the speaking of Spanish is the most overtly bombarded and excoriated Chicano cultural characteristic of them all. If so, it may very well explain the reason why it has generated the opposite response among brown Americans. Chicanos obviously cannot or will not relinquish their linguistic heritage.

The late Professor George I. Sanchez of New Mexico, a pioneer in bilingual studies, was convinced that the school's "obstinate persistence" to make English the only language among Mexican Americans had produced a bilingualism of wide qualitative range.[5] Hence, the language issue progressively developed and emerged as a class barrier or cactus curtain to deny Chicano and Spanish surname students equality with whites. It provided the ideal pretext to exclude "those Mexicans" from full fraternal partnership in the American experience in the southwestern United States.

Be that as it may, the sound development of linguistic skills is essential to personal progress in our democratic social milieu formatted in microcosm in the schools. Therefore, by legislative mandate the schools' curriculum is verbal-centered, a fact most Mexicans and Chicanos have long past conceded. Few, if any, brown Americans have ever challenged or questioned the ultimate goal of the schools to develop the English language proficiency of their children.

Most brown Americans recognize the reality that coherent self-expression and competence in English is central to good school progress and achievement. When, and if, conflict arises between the schools and

---

5. George I. Sanchez, "Spanish in the Southwest," *Unpublished mimeographed essay,* 1962.

the community, the root of the problem is often a question of the methodology applied, poor teaching techniques, or covert and overt demeaning of their children's language and culture. Harsh treatment and punishment for minor school violations is another source of much resentment and conflict.

One hundred and fifty years of first, limited, and then, antagonistic interaction between whites and brown Americans has generated little compromise or understanding for the latter in the schools. Most teachers and school administrators continue to possess an incredible lack of training, sensitivity, and an almost innate-like lack of desire to develop and implement a psychologically relevant methodology for teaching a marginal English-speaking or bilingual-bicultural group like the Chicano.

Conversely, decades of antagonistic monocultural and monolinguistic diffusion and confusion has produced and encouraged a distinctive bilingualism and biculturalism. Ironically, the Chicano by-product of this psychological and social encounter (and veil of ignorance), is presumed to be irreparable by the perpetrators themselves. Chicanos are viewed by many whites to be socially dysfunctional to such a degree that little hope remains that they can ever achieve full-fledged American acceptance.

NEGATIVE LEARNING AND ITS CONSEQUENCES

The uncompromising urgency to deprive and cleanse the student of first, his Mexican heritage and second, his linguistic handicap—in short, his symbolic world—is a form of desocialization that severely impairs a child's biosocial development. Some schools persist in pursuing an educationally unsound and psychologically unhealthy program by rejecting Spanish-speaking behavior on school grounds, and the time-tested general policy of Anglicizing the child's name, i.e., Jose to Joe, Juan to John, and Enrique to Henry continues. Moreover, the course of instruction includes pronouncing the pupil's Spanish surname (should he possess one), in phonetical English. "Altering the child's name," Chicano scholars allege, to "an acceptable American-sounding one" regardless of the psychological damage done to the child's self-image.

Little acumen is required to make the connection between the gradual desocialization and deprivation of brown children from their intimately personal linguistic world through punishment (frowns, etc.) and reward methods, and the stunting of their psychological growth. Brown children are deprived of any emotional attachment or sensitivity to their own names and to their racial identity. The aversive conditioning process through which they are channeled insidiously cultivates a psychological vacuum which not too curiously correlates with the brown child's nurturing of an antipathy for persons and objects of Mexican origin.

Following a course of instruction in which the child's desocialization and the substitution of new forms of behavior are a major goal, with a subsequent change in reference group, certain behavioral patterns become self-evident. First, brown children must surely possess substantial ego-strength and resilience to weather the constant assailment of their Spanish idiom and culture for as long as they do. Second, while it may seem to provide some youngsters with the necessary English language skills hoped for, the process is educationally unsound. Arresting and stunting a child's language motor skills—whatever the idiom—incurs a psychological loss. Third, the youngsters' self-worth and inner equilibrium is emphatically threatened. And finally, immeasurable negative fixation and belated deviant biosocialism sets in; often, to the extent that personality variation becomes pathological—i.e., the *bato loco* syndrome (street hoodlums). A Colorado-raised self-proclaimed *pocho* (a derogatory Mexican term for identifying Mexican Americans) cogently described his school experience as follows:

> Most of our teachers frankly regarded us as totally inferior. I still remember the galling disdain of my sixth grade teacher, whose constant mimicking of our heavily accented speech drove me to a desperate study of Webster's dictionary in the hope of acquiring a vocabulary larger than hers. Sadly enough, I succeeded only too well, and for the next few years I spoke the most ridiculous high-flown rhetoric in the Denver public schools. One of my favorite words was "indubitably," and it must have driven everyone mad. I finally got rid of my accent by constantly reciting "Peter Piper picked a peck of pickled peppers" with little round pebbles in my mouth. Somewhere I had read about Demosthenes.

> During this phase of my childhood the cultural tug-of-war known as "Americanization" almost pulled me apart. There were moments when I would identify completely with the gringo world [What could have been more American than my earnest high-voiced portrayal of

George Washington, however ridiculous the cotton wig my mother had fashioned for me?] then quite suddenly, I would feel so acutely Mexican that I would stammer over the simplest English phrase. I was so ready to take offense at the slightest slur against Mexicans but I would imagine prejudice where none existed. But on other occasions, in full confidence of my belonging, I would venture forth into social areas that I should have realized were clearly forbidden to little Chicanos from Curtis Park. The inevitable rebuffs would leave me floundering in self-pity; it was small comfort to know that other minority groups suffered even worse than we did.[6]

The public schools systematically subject Chicanos to a negative differential conditioning experience which, in effect, is a calculated proven design for failure as Chicanos by Chicanos; obviously, because the system's deculturation process hinders the natural course of cognitive development. Inescapably the school's firm and inflexible position for monocultural and monoracial development is at the heart of the problem. Simply stated, the means or process of separating youngsters from their parent culture and language substantially reduces general working ability. It coincidentally profoundly retards and reduces otherwise normal socialization to the dominant society and produces a sense of rejection. Inhibited aggression, melancholia, and retardation of critical faculties maturation is wrought by the schools' idea of an education for bicultural brown pupils.[7]

Historically, the public schools stand on what they consider a successful time-tested educational philosophy; specifically, their course of instruction, which militates against the sound implementation of minority group alternative concepts for education. Yet, with that mindset, and in that framework, teachers fruitlessly seek to actualize the accepted professional credo that successful responses should be impressed upon elementary schoolchildren; and, for expanding growth based on the foundations they bring to school. The idea is that a student's attention should be focused on tasks he can do rather than on tasks he cannot nor does not like to do.

---

6. Enrique P. Lopez, "A Hyphenated American Discovers He Can't Go Home Again," unpublished mimeograph, n.d.

7. "All that our parents teach us, all that we learn at home and in childhood. All that has cultural value, our language, religion, family, is denied us. Spanish becomes the language of failure since the English taught us is the language of success." Comments made by Professor Raul Ruiz, Mecha Central Conference, Pasadena, California, October, 1990.

What is overlooked in the course of instruction is the immense negative degree of frustration generated. While it is indispensable as an incentive to learning, long-term, uninterrupted, and intense frustration can be counterproductive and a cause for failure. Realistically, as any experienced educator will accede, this approach is not in keeping with the avowed philosophy and purpose of the American public school system which generally adheres to the principle that "a child should never be permitted to think of himself as a failure."

Brown children, like any normal children, need tasks at which they can succeed. Failure reduces self-esteem and the incentive to learn. Chicano children generally respond positively to instruction during the first two or three years in school. However, the evidence indicates that a mental block to learning, or negative learning, results as brown children are progressively alienated from their basic normative reference group and the psychological roots of their being. As their anxiety heightens and their biosocial motivation is interrupted, and as teachers continue to demand more positive results without progressive readiness, children acquire negative learning habits and, thereby, fail.

The first point of issue, therefore, is irrefutable; that is, that the schools are horrendously inept and unprepared for teaching Chicano students. Because of the institutions' primary concern with establishing new monocultural forms of behavior by way of social disintegration, and adverse socialization, the learning of the traditional so-called three "R's" is lost in the shuffle. Furthermore, the monocultural social curriculum is not compatible with the psychological condition demanded by poor brown children. More than half a century of proven failure is solid evidence that the schools' monoculturalism has failed in the educating of barrio brown American children. Only the brown group's augmented numbers, as well as its more pronounced urban profile, has given the intolerable condition an air of greater urgency in our times.

VERBALISM AND CONCEPTUAL THINKING

In our more enlightened age it is paradoxical and ironic to discover that in a democratic and republican society, psychological freedom or the inner power to will freely, is denied the smallest of our Chicano citizens. The reality and tragedy of the situation is truly one in which the brown child's intellect, while not positively strengthened and cultivated, is inhibited and directed from a normal pattern of maturation. The barrio Mexican American pupil is a defenseless victim of internal coercion of old established concrete parochial barriers which hinder his ability to act as a free brown American personality.

Another pervasive and generally ignored shortcoming is the failure of the schools to develop conceptual thinking for all students. Even college students often find themselves in the difficult position of withdrawing from the condition of being "spoon-fed." Too few students are motivated or trained to be critical thinkers. Basically this problem is rooted in the pseudo-thinking and verbal gymnastics experiences through which youngsters are programmed in the elementary and secondary schools. Since pseudo-learning is, in most cases, more accurately described as pure verbalism, children are generally guided and compelled to learn words they do not comprehend, rarely use or never use.

Ignoring the reality of the socially separate communities, barrio Chicanos are expected to accumulate middle-class English symbolic perceptual experiences in abundance through late adolescence. However, given the social curriculum, the methodology applied, the resultant biosocial retardation and consequent mental blocking, most never acquire a new healthy psychological point of reference. School policy, nonetheless, requires they progress at the same rate as Anglo middle-class children whose parent tongue is English and whose value systems constitute the core of the social curriculum in the school setting.

In spite of the growing evidence and the many problems we have elaborated upon above, many educators persist in their makeshift theory that bilingualism is a major retardation factor that restricts verbal mediation by Mexican American children. That such an antiquated educational posture persists, despite the fact it is common knowledge among linguists that children are capable of learning any language successfully, if sympathetically taught, has to be the most callous disregard of others' individual freedom in the libertarian United States.

With all this in mind, it is not particularly surprising that a professional educator–Chicano community "alternative education proposal" impasse has resulted which is principally due to a supremacist ideology rooted in monoculturalism and racial oppression. The Chicano counter that the issue goes beyond a simple chasm of language differences, or student inability is correct. Common sense suggests that if such were the case, it would have been resolved decades ago.

An undercurrent pervades white American culture and thought that "all Mexicans" (i.e., brown Americans too) hate white Americans.

The arrogant presumption that Chicanos waste themselves hating whites is unwarranted paranoia, a persistent legacy born of evil and unnatural national political inclinations and actions.[8] Ergo, the "Mexican" has got to be made less Mexican in order to free him of his hatreds. But this frame of thought also raises the question of "who, therefore, will liberate the whites from hating Mexicans?"

Nearly two generations of brown children have been introduced to the white Anglo world by way of television and film. This phenomenon has aided many of them linguistically, and brought them intimately in daily contact with the American Way of Life. The socio-psychological influence of television on the brown American, which most certainly is immense, remains a topic for further empirical study. There is little argument that television is a remarkable socializing instrument. It presents youngsters with non-barrio social experiences heretofore absent in the barrio setting of previous generations. Urbanization is another major environmental condition that has accelerated contact and social interaction between Chicanos and whites. Both of these conditions ideally help internalize and fortify language and social skills learned in school.

Nonetheless, urbanization, television, and the accented social interaction with majority group members notwithstanding, brown children remain handicapped because the schools fail to provide a realistic system of verbal mediation, thereby enabling the student to engage successfully in the complex symbolic thinking required in the school's academic format.

Professor Sanchez for many years recognized that the issues were "not truly linguistic ones, but rather ones in the area of social policy, of school administration, and of pedagogical competence." Sanchez was being kind, because this conviction is not totally unfounded. Many Chicano pupils begin to lose ground starting with grade three or four, although by this point most pupils have absorbed an extensive English

---

8. While it is common knowledge white Americans have generally held the darker races in contempt, the unconstitutional and humiliating relocation of Japanese Americans during World War II was comparable to the tyranny perpetrated against most tribal Americans, but particularly the Cherokee nations. Japan's expansionist conspiracies at the turn of the century mirrored those of the United States against Mexico in its movement to the Pacific. Naval actions in the Pacific, such as the leasing of ports, immigration into the country and neighboring countries, followed by calculated diplomacy and a successful surprise attack! Little wonder the government and the anti-yellow race peril alarmists and bigots "relocated" even old women and children.

vocabulary from a variety of sources including the school. By the time many brown pupils reach eighth grade they are, according to most studies, generally a year or more educationally behind because, for a variety of hidden reasons, they fail to keep up academically with their white Anglo peers.[9] White educators still allege they fall behind because they are learning English!

9. The "hidden reasons" are psychological. The school social curriculum is a barrier to academic learning and development. It disorients youngsters and paralyzes the natural development of their mental faculties.

CHAPTER 2

The Formative Years:

Desocialization and Alienation

*F*undamentally the core curriculum of the American public schools has a threefold objective. First, to monoculturalize and monoracialize young people in secular humanist idealism and subjective relativism whence develops their character.[10] Second, they are to be instructed in good citizenship, and finally, they are required to learn the three "R's." Thus, both the pupil end-product and by-product are basically determined by this format. In effect, it represents the proverbial educational means to an end.

Obviously, learning good citizenship and the three "R's" presents little problem for most students. Adapting to and incorporating the school's social curriculum, as the schools offer it, is another matter. An increasing number of scholars recognize that monocultural socialization in the schools deprives different ethnic groups, including Chicanos, of their psychological self-worth and of any positive cultural condition they might otherwise possess.

Non-white scholars strongly suggest the schools' social curriculum is particularly hostile and oppressive to colored minority children self-images and expectations. If that is the case, it is not too unreasonable to suggest that its negative impact is due to the fostering of colored

---

10. The inference here is that their Hispano Mexican or Chicano cultural self-worth and world view is inferior and not as worthy as the secular Anglo-American.

minority subservience and white American supremacy. Educators should not be surprised, therefore, to learn that brown students acquire a negative self-image very early in their school experience. Also, that brown children realize they are being guided and taught to fail as Chicanos, or as members of a colored minority. Surely, to suggest that failure breeds failure, once the cycle of failure is begun, is superfluous.

Even in so-called "Mexican schools" where Americanization and white success are less evident status symbols, and the learning of English language skills is of secondary importance or of no importance at all, the schools inculcate a failure and dropout syndrome by way of cultural disintegration and linguistic separation and deprivation. In addition, the primary guides and approbators of positive social behavior are white teachers and models. In schools where Chicanos compete with whites, brown students often develop a lack of self-confidence in English language skills, and acquire a more pronounced "low class" stigma because of their visible skin color and Mexican heritage. Realistically, it could not be otherwise given the antagonistic "anti-Mexican" monocultural social air of the schools. These problems and the psychological tensions associated with them are often heightened by frowning on Spanish usage on school grounds—a discriminatory practice that invariably accentuates the psychological armoring of Chicano students. The ultimate agenda aim has always been to strip the brown youngster's biosocial connection with Mexicanism. Separation from any operant knowledge of Spanish has no other positive educational purpose. So, antipathy for the brown child's cultural heritage and race is insidiously inculcated and reinforced.

When the youngster subliminally, or even instinctively, presumes that his Mexicanness is rejected, and that school personnel and white peers are hostile to him and his ethnicity, he withdraws or develops a mental block to positive learning. Intelligent brown children learn to forget materials that are threatening to their self-esteem, or antagonistic to basic cultural attitudes [religious values and language]. But they also set up barriers to general learning. In the process these children progressively refine their repression as they chronologically mature. And, as the repression becomes progressively more subconscious, determination of the cause for failure becomes equally difficult to ascertain. Quite naturally, noticeable behavioral change takes many forms.

For example, incoherent and monosyllabic English speech patterns are cues that something is wrong.[11] Diffidence and a disinclination to conversation, or boisterous conduct, are common traits among brown students who have suffered great psychological damage, often due to the multiple interruptions of natural biosocial maturation. In place of disoriented social skills, partly eroded as a result of the school's uncompromising monolingual and monocultural school setting, many youngsters plateau prematurely. Many of these children develop functional linguistic patterns consisting of individualized idioms. Multiplying evidence on these issues leaves little doubt that the schools retard and corrupt the basic mental and psychological development of brown children.

Brown youngsters learn to feel inferior linguistically, culturally, religiously, and racially. Moreover, their social skills are inalterably shattered and disrupted. For whatever inferences such a disintegrated personality may draw, or whatever inventiveness he may have developed, it is generally not as a Chicano but as a non-Chicano.[12] First, because he has had to arrive at these analyses through mental processes using an English vocabulary to which he is conditioned; and, which to him is not psychologically relevant. Second, the basic types of mental problems presented in school are unrelated to, or have little connection with his cultural or psychological condition; finally, because educational psychologists concur that mental problems cannot be solved through reading.

If, indeed, relational thinking is dependent in large measure on the ability to express relations by means of verbal symbols, then, it logically follows that the best approach to teaching Chicanos to develop this skill would be to teach them in a language or cultural climate to which they can relate, or in which they already function, i.e., a bicultural Mexican American one.

---

11. Considerable reinforcement of poor language skills occurs because this pre-matured plateau level has become the emotionally accepted mode of communication for the street thugs and hoodlums. Any motivation to develop improved linguistic skills has long been forsaken by confused and psychologically impaired children whose initial withdrawal is simply an attempt to escape from the impact of social disintegration stimulation.

12. See Robert Rosenthal and Lenore Jacobson, *"Pygmalion in the Classroom"* (New York: Holt, Rinehart and Winston, Inc, 1987), pp. 47–66.

THE BROWN COMMUNITY AND THE SCHOOLS

Time-honored and sanctioned social custom in concert with the nativism spawned by the country's secular humanism system are major causes for resistance to vital bilingual education programs in the Southwest. Invariably the legislation favorably supportive of bilingualism stems from ulterior political motives rather than from any educational or democratic principle. However, far more discouraging is the pervasively blatant educational insensitivity, or lack of concern, among policy-making individuals who hold the reins to actuate progressive and positive change. In this regard, the Los Angeles City Schools, considered by many educators to be one of the best systems in the country, is a notable example of a large urban system traditionally guided by a Board of Education with a narrow political and insensitive educational philosophy.

By 1970 the dropout rate among Chicanos in Los Angeles City Schools, was at its lowest level—just slightly over sixty percent! Yet, a few years earlier in March, 1963, when the Chicano dropout rate was closer to seventy percent, members of the Los Angeles Board of Education rejected any suggestion that a bilingual and bicultural student group with special needs and problems existed in the district![13] Furthermore, the Los Angeles Board of Education in collusion with its school administrators was instrumental in generating resistance to the now defunct Casey Bill.

The Casey Bill was a California educational mandate that required foreign language instruction in grades six, seven, and eight [primarily Spanish]. The Casey Bill was a unique diverse cultural legislative mandate, which at the time presented unforeseen long range goals for cultivating and improving rapport between white and brown Americans, simply by bridging the so-called linguistic gap. Abrogation of the Casey Bill occurred in 1965.[14]

---

13. "Social and Educational Problems of Rural and Urban Mexican American Youth." *Summary of the proceedings of the Annual Southwest Conference,* April 16, 1963, Los Angeles, California. Information Kit, p. 5.

14. In 1964, 30,000 students in the Los Angeles City Schools alone were studying Spanish and the school district anticipated 80,000 by the end of 1985. One observer wrote that the legislation was passed "as a political gesture to Spanish-speaking Californians who incidentally don't need the instruction!" See the *Van Nuys News,* July 10, 1964.

Whatever criticism may be forthcoming from opponents, the fact remains that the social curriculum, and linguistic relevance, are central to teaching children. For some reason the overriding reality of need is still resisted. Prior to the desegregation of California's public schools in 1947, "Mexican School" administrators and teachers held school social events, and adhered to linguistic policies far more suitable for teaching Mexicans than is presently officially required.[15] More realistic commitment to practicality, and to the true purpose of educating children from a specific ethnic background, was evidently more appreciated in the past. Perhaps it was more feasible, given the vast number of immigrants that entered the United States at the turn of the century, and the then socially accepted school policy of segregating colored minority children.

In many areas of the Southwest school officials and teachers presented plays either in Spanish, or at least bilingually, for the benefit of the Spanish-speaking community. Community interest and response was energetic and enthusiastic, judging from the large number of adults who attended them. In review, this more relevant educational approach, while on a limited scale, forged a solid bridge between the schools and the barrio community. Parents, students, and school personnel, respectively, gained socially and professionally from these school ethnic-oriented functions.[16]

Learning for youngsters is all-encompassing. Most educators concur with the adage that the child's home environment should be an integral and formal part of that experience. In this regard one of the best, most recent examples of articulating a school program inclusive of barrio life was recorded in 1963.

In Merced, California, Spanish was used to teach Spanish-speaking students on the intermediate level. The positive results were astonishing. School teachers and officials discovered that student morale

---

15. Charles Wollenberg, "Mendez vs. Westminister: Race, Nationality and Segregation in California Schools," *California Historical Quarterly,* (LIII, Winter, 1974), pp. 317–330. This case confirms that "Segregation . . . foster antagonisms in the children and suggests inferiority among them where none exists." See also "Spanish-Speaking Peoples," *U.S. Commission on Civil Rights,* February 5, 1964.

16. Sal Castro, a Los Angeles High School teacher, was criticized and later transferred from one high school to another within the Los Angeles School District, for promoting bilingual and Spanish-speaking functions of this nature in the 1960s. His sensitivity for Chicano and Mexican student needs was threatening to the status quo. The "ethnic stuff had to go."

improved, and that the usually apathetic working-class brown community was highly receptive. In fact, one teacher reported that on the day her class presented a Spanish play, great-grandparents, grandparents, and parents, persons who rarely attended school affairs, were present. The professional consensus was that students were ready and willing to speak Spanish, sentiments that reflected pride in achievement.[17]

Unfortunately, American public schools persist in rigid monocultural conformist policies that have generally proven to be counterproductive. Non-white adult products of this "false" American negative school experience, like Mexican Americans, learn to skip public school functions. Why? Because an irreversible and effective negative cyclical social pattern was set in motion among them many years before by oppressive and un-American standard school policies. The memory of the thinly veiled humiliation they were processed through because they were Mexican dies hard.

Schools cannot effectively operate a psychologically healthy and progressive school program without strong parental and community support. Consequently, the absence of a substantial bridge between school and home encourages and fuels the historical social gap or void in the children's educational and emotional experience. Devoid of community support or social relevancy, the school setting stands as an alien cultural and hostile fact in the barrio. Moreover, counter-cultural barrio life is strengthened and reinforced as a viable separate enclave to the general mainstream, due to insensitivity and persistent hostile school policies.

Even a cursory inspection of school policies serving barrio children indicates the schools are a long way from resolving the simple cultural problem and language learning processes of Mexican and Chicano pupils. Reluctance by school officials, legislators, and teachers to support a more realistic diverse social curriculum, and more thought out methods of instruction in the education of brown American youngsters has created a formidable impasse.

Without appearing redundant, it must be stressed that although bilingualism is central to educating some Mexican and barrio Chicanos, it represents only one solution to correcting one cause for failure among brown American students. But whatever the case may be, the suppres-

---

17. *California Education,* Vol. I, November, 1963.

sion or rejection of bilingualism, biculturalism, and a brown American self-identity fuels the antagonism and fosters much bitterness between Chicanos and whites. Chicanos hardly cherish the idea that Spanish and their Hispano-Mexican heritage be considered socially undesirable and inferior. To expect members of this group to bend to such narrow dictum given their historical precedence in the Southwest, and the fact they live in a free society, is abusive administrative and school board policy.[18]

While it may be partially true that bilingual programs have been successfully developed and implemented in a number of sectors of the Southwest, it is also true the majority of them have been short-lived. Most have been of a pilot nature with little long-term benefit for brown American students. Indeed, within those states which have grudgingly adopted bilingual programs, the academic and social impact on students will probably not be notably observable for at least a generation. Efforts to eliminate them, however, are constant and unrelenting.

18. See comments by Professor Raul Ruiz on page 6 in chapter 1.

CHAPTER 3

Mexican Stereotypes:

A Basis of Hostility

*D*esocialization and cultural disintegration are insidious biosocial alienating and debilitating monocultural processes that have received adequate treatment in studies of other American minority groups. However, no comparable historical experience to the host brown American community experience of the Southwest which was incorporated into the American union by war of conquest exists. The resident tribal peoples, the so-called Indians were either victims of government sanctioned genocide or physically relocated in reservations. In short, they were brought under control and were made dependent on the whims of a hostile federal government. So, the Chicano pattern of cultural disequilibrium is analogous to the European immigrant experience, but only insofar as present-day monocultural processing and deculturation is concerned.[19]

Moreover, it should be borne in mind that European cultures are considered positive old world heritages. Hence, general disinheritance of Europeans requires no racial disavowal, shame, or inferiority due to skin color. The Eurocentric white mental framework does not harshly denounce the "mother" of the United States, nor its "cousins" like

---

19. Linda Chavez, *Out of the Barrio* (New York: Basic Books), pp. 161–165, supports the defunct fairy-tale immigrant analogy that perpetuates Chicano foreignness and nourishes gullible white American racist sentiments, thereby, making the Chicano victim guilty of the crime perpetrated on him by generations of a white American social custom of racial separation.

France and Germany. Even Christopher Columbus is a good guy, almost American, when he is not being used as a symbol to bash Spain and Roman Catholicism with hate inciting Black Legend allegations.

Chicano children who initially enter elementary school with a positive self-image, and a normal and healthy degree of self-confidence, discover a school setting that is hostile to both their race and ethnicity. When the school demands uncompensated debilitating racial and ethnic concessions, they are trapping these pupils in a psychological and social environment over which they have no control. They are being culturally and emotionally subordinated and changed forever. Elementary school age children are incredibly responsive and able to handle personal conflict and environmental complexity in the early grades. Ergo, which in great part helps explain why they internalize whatever mental conflict may develop during their negative processing experience.

Thus, these children do not overtly rebel when their name is changed from Jose to Joe. Nor do they resist when their surnames are Anglocized. They also may elicit little concern when their eating habits and diet are programmed differently. So it would seem. But the insensitive and inadequate educational methodology utilized, and the monocultural, white race glorification and exclusive social environment notwithstanding, the schools are no longer the singular alienating cause.

Mexican stereotypes on television and film in animated cartoons and plays have become more widespread in the past generation. Pre-school children are still exposed to Mexican caricatures which are as harmful as they are unreal. Children internalize these models many years before they personally encounter them in school books and other materials.[20] Whereas in the past the schools perpetuated stereotypes through indiscriminate selection of textbooks and prejudiced teachers, we find that the major traditional disseminators of anti-Mexican sentiments are now supported by the media and film. The cycle is simple: television or film introduce negative images and concepts, and the schools reinforce them. Both are guilty of systematically cultivating and

---

20. Frankly, one of the major goals of the Chicano movement was to destroy the then-popular caricature and offensive stereotypes of Mexicans. See chapter 8 passim. See also James Patterson and Peter Kim, *The Day America Told the Truth: What People Really Believe about Everything That Really Matters* (New York: Prentice Press, 1991), p. 124.

disseminating negative notions and anti-Mexican propaganda. Cultural disequilibrium, bruised egos, and the basis for a brown marginal personality find considerable root here.

Barrio Chicano youngsters are often psychologically prepared by older siblings, neighborhood chums, and parents to participate and accept certain changes in their initial school experience. Thus, brown American children learn they must live two identities—at home a youngster is called Juan and at school he is named John. In the process they learn and cultivate many non-Chicano social attitudes, mannerisms, and patterns of behavior. Since normal and intelligent children want to be accepted, respected, and loved, they find it expedient to leave their "Mexican ways" at home. Thus, they avoid rejection and reduce ridicule opportunities appreciably by their white peers and teachers.[21]

Finally, the schools' social program to uplift Chicano children, and the pupils' innate desire for approbation, combine to transform many Spanish surname children into aspiring brown Anglos with all its negative ramifications. These influences should not be minimized because once these psychological impulses and substitute patterns of behavior are impressed on young minds, eradicating or supplanting them in later years is frankly impossible.

LEARNING THE BANDIDO ROLE

In elementary school where biosocialization begins in earnest, black and white children quite naturally identify with their respective racial groups. The Mexican American child has no American reference group with which to identify, so he identifies with things Mexican. Although it is not in school where all children learn for the first time that they are different, it is in school where they learn that some, like themselves, are accorded different treatment because of their skin color.

Moreover, because they choose to identify with Mexican persons and things, they acquire a foreign label and false self-image very early. Their peers cue into what they perceive as the brown American's familiar reference group from the animated cartoons and movies seen on

---

21. The Little Schools of 400 developed by Felix Tijerina in the 1950s in Texas, and Head Start programs of the 1970s, sought to acquaint brown children with the social and cultural environment of the Anglo schools they were to attend. See Guadalupe San Miguel, *"Let All of Them Take Heed: "Mexican Americans and the Campaign for Educational Equality in Texas."* 1910–1981 (Austin: University of Texas Press, 1987), pp. 140–151.

their home television sets. In this manner the framework for the brown American to see himself and to be seen by others as a Mexican is actuated, and firmly fixed in both cultural experiences.[22]

Frankly, all the combined stereotypical Mexican characteristics of a brown, dirty, lazy, cruel *bandido* Mexican type are still the Mexican reference group with which all brown children and their peers are impressed.[23] Although a mature mind may find it difficult to understand why a Chicano child would choose to identify with a bandit-type, a child needs to identify with something. A *bandido* image is far superior to no image at all.

The real problem is an absence of publicly acclaimed brown American heroes in American society and in school. Many brown children assume a Mexican tough guy, bad guy and negative reference group by default. Moreover, it is in school where they learn to be harsh, to be mean-spirited, to be insensitive and callous to parental sensitivities, and to the feelings of others. For many brown youngsters human life begins to lose its positive value.[24]

In the years of social development and maturation that follow, the children's role-playing skills are polished. They become more overt and apropos in the intermediate school years, when youngsters begin to expand their self-images and personalities from the primary setting of home and the school. A socially deviant point of reference also becomes more evident. The hostile and anti-social demeanor of *cholo* [bum] and *bato loco* [street hoodlums] youths, and the belligerent raccoon-like masks donned by brown girls, reflects two mental conditions: (1) the out-group, tough, resistant, defensive role-playing the brown student has actualized to sustain his self-respect and honor, and (2) a rejected, psychologically damaged individual who craves for white authority figure attention and approbation.

---

22. Patterson and Kim, *The Day America Told The Truth, Loc. Cit.,* p. 124.

23. This methodical negative socialization is taken for granted by most persons, teachers, and parents alike. But, it is the beginning of objectifying of Chicanos and brown American children as foreign images. Indeed, even the Anti-Defamation League of B'nai B'rith charged that the brown American mostly "has replaced the black as the 'invisible American.'" See *Los Angeles Times,* May 17, 1970.

24. Professor Julian Nava after a dozen years of observation from within the Los Angeles School Board of Education noted that the schools are greatly responsible for the formation of negative self-images, hostile behavior, and callousness among Chicanos. See KTLA *Pacesetters* Interview with Ray Gonzales, 1978.

In the 1940s, urban Chicanos emulated movie film tough guy characters like the "Dead-End Kids," because of the former's association with the latter's impoverished social environment, and the social deviance characterization reference of the actors. In retrospect, the connection surely must have met a psychological group reference need because it closely resembled the assumed Mexican bandit self-image of many brown Americans.

The singular bandit or tough guy image or role is open to the brown youngster as a traditional vehicle for objectifying a corrupted self-identity, as well as for expressing his feelings of solitude and rebellion. In this biosocial developmental process, the child may coincidentally manifest symptoms of hostility spawned by an institutionalized experience of rejection and feelings of unworthiness. Among brown students this behavior may be notably overt by the later elementary school years. But ascertaining the origin of their hostility and subdued repression can be difficult at this point.

All normal youngsters desire and need the ego-satisfaction required to develop stable and mentally healthy personalities. To be a loser in a highly competitive society, or in the social milieu of a school environment which mirrors the values and attitudes of that society, can be ego-deflating and psychologically painful. The ultimate tenets of monocultural secular humanist conformity, as currently modeled and presented in the schools, are set for coercing Chicano students into, (1) relinquishing their racial and cultural identity, and (2) unrealistically transforming their mental references into white Anglo-Saxon republican protestant ones.

MONOCULTURAL SUPREMACISM

This monocultural process or melting pot supremacism is not restricted to colored persons of Mexican ancestry. Rather, all non-white and "un-American" ethnics are presumed to be inferior and un-American until they prove themselves. The diminution of self-determination among colored Americans is both the result and purpose of this processing. In effect, the mechanics of promised equality and inclusion into the American mainstream is so well refined, and so insidiously impressed that many colored Americans permanently lose their inherent Constitutional right "to be" and "to will freely" without being aware of it.

At issue here is the irreversible loss of normal psychological growth as colored Americans. That ideal is stunted and corrupted because healthy development of colored American self-worth is denied them. Moreover, since their true racial self-image is distorted, and in many cases lost, they are also no longer free in any fundamentally conceived sense of the word. Now, since in fact the vast majority of the colored minority population cannot be totally socially monoculturalized or disorganized and deculturated, alternative roles for the more resistant and dissident have been defined.

For example, the established alternative role guidance for brown American children is to teach and encourage them to identify with a non-American or foreign group. In the schools' subjective relativist agenda and social curriculum they are unofficially identified and labeled as Hispanics or Mexicans. Ergo, the psychologically incapacitating success of this method of conditioning or socialization is remarkably time-tested. Consequently, the reference group identification, and the social organization that ensues, can best be described as a pernicious form of psychological apartheid. It is not by chance that this occurs.

Few persons can endure the tension and anxiety of continuous differential conditioning and repeated rejection without noticeable psychological impairment. Anger and frustration are the initial expressions of heightened negative social pressures. Little wonder Chicano and Mexican parents are often alarmed at the disquieting substitute patterns of *gabacho* (Anglo) dissident and rebellious behavior they observe in their children. They see a distinctive behavior devoid of ethnic pride coupled with a marked egocentric individualization; and more painful, a strong sense of alienation from the restraints of parental discipline and cultural direction.

More closely examined, a consistent but tragic scenario unfolds as the schools' program of subjective relativism and aversive conditioning takes hold. It can be described as a condition that energizes a powerful psychological chasm between many brown children and their parents. Gradually, however inevitably, a crisis point is reached in the middle school years; principally because pupils are better able to defend themselves more adequately at that age. Although still guided by keen and youthful unrestrained emotions, middle school level pupils are perceptibly more outspoken and direct in their social interactions with others.

Nonetheless, the schools inordinately guide the children to choose between their host culture and the conflicting institutional subjectivistic values and social direction of the monocultural Anglo school ambience. That a choice of such psychological magnitude must be made is lamentable enough. But a serious crisis is reached. Preference by youngsters for the intimate and real world of home and Chicanismo is only natural. Yet, it is no mean decision or growth experience for a youngster. Their choice to remain marginally free is prudent; this in order to retain a semblance of self-respect and personal integration. Surely, the choice must come after considerable agonizing. Obviously, because it is totally one stratagem to get the kid out of the barrio, but how do you get the barrio out of the kid?

The following two chapters will touch upon the junior high or middle school experience, pubescence, and the psycho-social phenomenon known as adolescence; and, how it relates to the Mexican American heritage and to the making of the brown American consciousness and self-image.

CHAPTER 4

The Early Adolescent Years:

Self-Images and Expectations

*T*he congenial blend of secular humanist egoism and the capitalist work ethic leads to an exaggerated emphasis on competition, materialism, and a worship of achievement. Granted, it approaches a state of mind which can ultimately be described as one which makes a "fetish of success." Most majority culture oriented students are guided and nurtured in this direction, simply because these are American monocultural social curricular and extracurricular social expectations. Brown Americans generally lack this fetish-like majority group point of reference. Hence, because they are not as socially aware or challenged in the same manner, they do not respond like whites. In addition, they are not expected by their teachers and peers to strive toward these goals.

Besides, given the popular stereotypes that Mexicans are mentally deficient, non-achievers, and lazy, most teachers expect Chicanos to be non-achievers, not uncommonly refusing to recognize that they are simply unfamiliar with majority group competitive expectations.[25] The very idea that brown pupils require academic socialization like everybody else is never honestly considered. Also, an inordinate general consensus among teachers that it doesn't do any good to try to motivate

---

25. The term "Mexican" in quotation marks in this study refers to the white American's erroneous perception and identification of a brown American as a foreigner based on the latter's skin color and Spanish surname. In Southwestern American society "Mexican" means "brown."

"Mexicans," ordinarily begets the expected negative or unproductive results from the latter.[26]

Now, since a non-creative person is invariably a non-achiever, it follows that a non-achiever cannot be expected to be a successful person. After years of aversive conditioning, cultural disintegration, and deprivation, many Chicano youngsters actually believe they are, in fact, inferior and develop the attitudes of non-achievers too. Once vented, this attitude progressively leads to low self-worth and a general lack of confidence, lethargy, or dullness; traits that too often become characteristically evident among brown youngsters.

Moreover, under present conditions traditionally the hero and success models presented to children in learning materials continue to be clean-cut, God-fearing, materially successful white Americans. What did a Mexican *bandido* and loser ever accomplish anyway? Successful Chicanos and persons of Mexican ancestry, Chicanos say with justification, are "white-washed" and ascribed a Spanish or Hispanic label. Deplorable as it may be, the value and worth of whiteness continues to be stressed and reinforced while that of Mexicanness (i.e., brownness) is neglected or demeaned. To be Spanish-speaking, Catholic, and Mexican is not good. That is the differential socialization process young immature minds are forced to endure.

Countless books, treatises, and articles have been researched, written, and published regarding the critical importance of motivating children in a school setting. Prospective teachers are presented with the most recent theories of motivating children to be mentally healthy and high achievers. Frankly, it is a proud teacher who will relate tales of success in motivating an unusually unresponsive pupil which resulted in positive behavioral change and growth. This deep-rooted and selfless desire to help others comprises the inner constitution of many teachers, and it is a real source of inspiration for many high achievers. However, many teachers also prefer not to work with slow learners.

Since Chicanos are stereotyped as slow learners, few teachers concern themselves with members of this minority unless they are required to teach them. Furthermore, under the present institutional structure most teachers are generally unable to give adequate special attention to

---

26. This often expressed negative sentiment by teachers makes Jaime Escalante's success teaching so-called "Mexican" youngsters in East Los Angeles that much more remarkable. He proved them wrong. See also Rosenthal and Jacobson, *Pygmalion in the Classroom*, pp. 55–60.

troubled pupils due to large unmanageable class size, curriculum limi- tations, course content requirements, and an over-abundance of paper- work; most of which serves only the interest of placating bureaucrats and administrators with impermeable, dulled sensitivities who are all too often hideously oblivious of the real necessities of a true education.

An unmotivated child rarely finds any immediate value in school- work. In such a case, the probability is great the learning climate will not lend itself to a significant degree of intellectual growth. Given these con- ditions, a pupil cannot be expected to be as attentive and as academically energetic as is needed to satisfy the teacher and possibly his parents.

THE DUAL PARENT CONFLICT OF CHICANO CHILDREN

Teachers are legal parent substitutes, as well as competing parent mod- els. Theoretically, teachers are supposed to represent ideal adult goal models in growth for children. Therefore, *"in loco parentis"* is far more than just a legal concept. Teachers are mother or father with the capac- ity to reward or punish, to love or not to love. It is beyond academic debate that in ego—ideal formations, and personal integration, the teacher is, next to immediate family members, the most important fac- tor. No other adults are so trusted and given such vital control of their children by loving parents; particularly at such a critical stage in the child's growth and development.

Ironically, the most often heard parental comment, uttered by dis- traught brown parents at their children's disrespectful behavior is, *"Eso es lo que aprendes en la escuela?"* (Is that what you learn at school?), succinctly pinpoints a major source of the personal psychological dis- integration of Chicano children. It sets in motion a cultural conflict condition which is but a by-product of contradicting and competitive parental modeling and upbringing. The children are caught in the mid- dle, between two models and two loyalties. Normally between loving biological parents and often unkind, rejecting, distant generally white substitute parents, whose commendation they also desire.[27] Children

---

27. A kind of absent father familial condition exists in elementary school where the great major- ity of the teachers are females. According to some psychologists, forms of disturbed behavior "are far more common among boys, boy delinquents outnumber girls about five to one." Indeed, the allegations that a cause of disorder among boys, especially criminality, is rebellion and aggres- sion, as compensation for passivity and identification with the opposite sex (teachers) can be sub- stantiated. See Patricia Cayo Sexton, *The Feminized Male: Classrooms, White Collars and the Decline of Manliness* (New York: Vintage Books, 1970), pp. 7–9.

are overwhelmed by such a formidable cross cultural conflict and disharmony.

In addition, they are expected to overcome the formidable task of learning to be "good boys" or "good girls" in two competing clashing social environments. In the process the child's ego strength suffers because it is unable to easily resolve the conflict. Any degree of failure here reduces the child's self-esteem and control. Anxiety and guilt bruise and weaken the ego, which in turn leads to an appreciable loss of self-esteem and self-worth. For all accounts, the children's social condition is comparable to a broken home environment, wherein a once structured world progressively disintegrates; and, as a hypothetical divorce or separation looms, the anticipated emotional preference for one parent, and that parent's lifestyle, over the other forms.

In this connection, research cites a growing emotional distance between brown children and white teachers as youngsters grow in awareness of the racially discriminating treatment accorded them. Lost in their own ethos, it is natural for white teachers to favor white and brown Anglo-like children. Seemingly unimportant and unrecognized discriminatory practices of this nature inculcate clear-cut impressions in the Chicano mind. First, that Chicanos do not deserve or merit the attention of white children or teachers; second, it reinforces the brown student's belief that Chicanos are inferior as naturally as the white is superior. Thus, learning overriding emotional reasons to aspire to be white, reasons that are insidiously inculcated during the Chicano youngsters' formative years.[28]

Brown children realize some teachers do not appreciate them because they are Mexicans, but the idea of what a Mexican is, is an abstraction to these youngsters. In fact, most of their teachers view them as Mexicans only because they have brown skins or Spanish surnames. Understandably, then, many Chicanos mature with the false impression they are unappreciated because of some physical or mental imperfection or defect; or, because they are foreign Mexicans when in actuality they are only of Mexican descent. The malevolent pervasive current

---

28. Teachers and Students Report v. Mexican American Education Study. A Report of the United States Commission on Civil Rights, Washington DC, 1973, pp. 23–27. Since the school's social curriculum remains the same it is highly doubtful racial attitudes have changed. Some Mexican American scholars in their erroneous belief that Mexican Americans constitute "a separate class of whites throughout the Southwest . . ." See Guadalupe San Miguel, "Let All of Them Beware . . ." (Austin: University of Texas Press, 1990), p. 178.

notion that they belong to a despised conquered brown-skinned, non-European, anti-white American and culturally different group escapes them, because it is unfathomable to innocent children. Unfortunately, the conflicting condition undermines development of their natural capacities all the more because of its vicious insidiousness.

Most normal children seek and cherish a teacher's approbation. That aspiration is fully manifest in a pupil's emulation of the teacher's mannerisms, attitudes, and values. And, just as readily and unquestionably, they learn what this respected authority model figure may wish to convey to them. Children have enormous ego need gratification. They intuitively sense how adults feel about them, which explains the reason children's responses are more predictable than are adults.

DENIAL OF THE NATURAL RIGHT "TO BE"

Neighborhood primary schools in which the greater majority of the students are of Hispano Mexican background afford little opportunity for Chicanos to compete and socially interact with non-Chicanos. In some cases the junior high or middle school enhances the opportunity for social interaction with a diversity of white types and a more pragmatic and challenging student environment. However, larger classes, extra teacher loads, and the complexity of teaching at the intermediate school level drastically reduce opportunities for sorely needed individual student counseling. In addition, it requires that brown students become accustomed to less personalized attention. The psychologically damaged brown pupil is forgotten just at the point when there still remains a reasonable chance of salvaging his self-esteem by working sensibly and diligently to keep him in school.

Because the brown American community is presently in the throes of cultural transition, therefore, and severely culturally fractured, to accurately assess the degree of cultural alienation and the sense of rejection children experience by the time they leave elementary school is made more difficult. We can correctly assess, judging from the high dropout rate at the secondary school level, that the great majority are in an embryonic stage of dysphoria, cultural alienation, and socialized to fail after only six years of the affecting world of the public schools. It is not unreasonable to postulate that by age twelve most brown children have assumed irreversible negative self-images pertaining to their race, cultural heritage, and religion. Many youngsters are convinced they are inferior by this chronological age. Resignation to failure and social exclusion represent only two well-learned negative attitudes in the schools, via subtle monocultural indoctrination and differential social conditioning. At a time in human growth and development when a positive self-identity and cultivated ego-strength is critical, brown youngsters generally find themselves stripped of any. Thus, by this early stage the roots for a potential drop out and sit-in have been firmly set.

Be that as it may, in the realm of social and psychological reality, potential Chicano sit-ins and dropouts are pupils who have successfully learned to turn off the monolingual, monocultural, and aversive learning agenda by the time they leave sixth grade. Besides, the natural unwillingness of many to compromise their Chicano and Mexican Catholic Christian values and ideals beyond reasonable accommodation plateaus and paralyzes the original driving quest to learn and to progress academically. The secular humanist oriented school program, the demand for substitute behavior patterns, and the hostile anti-Mexican social curriculum, nurtures extreme forms of debilitating marginalism and inertia among a large percentage of the brown American student population.

At this educational juncture, a twelve-year-old child's negative and defiant behavior spawned by cultural disintegration, a school program fixed on changing the student's psychology and normative ideals, are still amendable through remediation or balance. This means that what the elementary school has succeeded in achieving through a program of cultural deprivation and social exclusion, the junior high school can still harmonize and amend.[29]

Children's behavioral patterns are more flexible than adults since they are more responsive to learning positive or correct forms of conduct and behavior, if guided in realistic and innovative directions. Since severely antagonized and frustrated youngsters are agonizing from a lack of self-esteem, because their normative ideals and self-worth have been shaken, degraded and reshaped; then, educators still possess the

---

29. The early educational background of a former Deputy Mayor of Los Angeles, 1975–1990, Grace Montanez Davis, is revealing. "In public schools, I just remember that we didn't learn anything. Because in those days we minorities were not expected to achieve—especially women . . . But Sacred Heart School, I was a Mexican girl who had a soul, and I had a mind, and the sisters developed it . . . So my academic training was fabulous. Plus, the one thing I've always said I received from my Catholic education was discipline. The discipline to apply myself to anything." *Los Angeles Tidings,* January 29, 1993.

opportunity and the responsibility to mollify the conflict and anxiety condition resultant of child abuse. Not to mention the immeasurable compensation due them for the gross injustice of violating these brown pupils' civil and natural right "to be." The intermediate high school years present the schools with the ideal time and place for this gainful purpose.

CHAPTER 5

The Middle School:

A Chicano Crossroads

*O*ne of the major functions and aims of the intermediate school or junior high school is to help children bridge the educational and emotional ladder between elementary school and senior high school. In the more highly industrialized regions of the urban United States, the junior high school has, as intended, lessened the socialization and maturation process pressures of students entering the more complex and competitive senior high school environment. Fundamentally, elementary schools prepare children to enter the intermediate school, and the latter prepares them for the social and academic rigors of senior high school.

Logically, the junior and senior high school academic and social programs builds on the fundamentals learned in elementary school. Emphasis on English skills and monocultural secular humanist middle class values and attitudes are progressively accentuated with substantial focus on college preparation and academic training. Moreover, in contrast to a neighborhood primary school setting or condition, dominant group values and attitudes become more actual and critical in the student's daily school experience. At this crossroads, chances are greatly enhanced Chicanos will meet "textbook ideal type" white middle-class youngsters whom they are being guided to copy or emulate by their educators and regulated school social custom.

It is apropos to note that most youngsters entering seventh grade have well-grounded preconceived notions about what constitutes the American ideal. Furthermore, by this grade level fashionable and culturally acquired stereotypical images of minorities have been permanently rooted. Since, at this point of psychological development and maturation, pupils become more overtly self-centered and conscious of their physical appearance and social status, biological or racial differences assume greater importance in their personal daily lives and in their social interaction with others.

Traditional major prerequisites for being American, fixed in immature and pliable minds, has meant being white and Anglo-Saxon. All references to being an American, henceforth, are based on that primitive, yet somber supremacist premise. With this in mind youngsters, therefore, can hardly be expected to think of Chicanos, Asians, and blacks as ideally American. Socially popular and shadowy anti-colored and anti-Mexican (i.e., anti-brown) sentiments cultivated in the American ethos are over-powering. Naturally, insofar as colored minorities are personally concerned, these attitudes assume their most profound and immoderate disparaging emotional expression in early adolescent school social interacting experiences.

More emphatically, ethnic and racial hostility surfaces more dramatically during the junior high school years than at any other period. Among white youngsters, culturally inbred anti-Mexican attitudes spawn irreversible negative social responses toward persons of Mexican origin. Social rejection and ostracism by one's peers and fellows during adolescence is an emotionally traumatic experience. In addition, the transitional adolescent ego-equilibrium of most teens cannot endure constant frustration and adversity with the finesse and adroitness of an experienced and hardened adult. Irrational and violent behavior on school campuses is invariably a by-product of the socially debilitating and traumatic social experience just described.

Nevertheless, given the chronological stage of adolescent emotional maturation, there is little question that for most Chicanos the intermediate school presents the last and best educational opportunity for the rebuilding and harmonizing of self-images and confidence generally undermined and notably shaken in grade school.

Normal chronological creativity and mental activity has been sufficiently repressed and reorganized by the time the brown child enters senior high school, to require personal attention. Unmitigated frustration wrought by repressive school policies and administrators, generates anti-social and defiant conduct which results in progressively harsher repressive measures. Motivational and guidance situations become more difficult. While it may be true that anxiety and intellectual capacities function together, a Chicano student's constant anxiety and growing defiance impairs and retards his intellectual growth and biosocial maturation.

According to Civil Rights Commission studies done in the past two decades, the culmination of the brown pupil's valiant and unappreciated struggle to retain a semblance of his self-esteem, integrity, and identity all too often finds resolution during the intermediate or high school years, at the age of sixteen or seventeen, when he or she prematurely leaves school.[30]

Among teachers it is common knowledge student-oriented colleagues often appreciate and find delight in teaching at the intermediate level, because for many it can be a truly satisfying and rich experience. Given the positive general disposition of teachers, and the youngsters' impressionable and uncorrupted biosocial stage, mutual positive responses are subsequently natural. But, often the middle school pupil's lack of sophistication and general untactful behavior stings in its trite denigration of others, particularly when thoughtless words are directed at the psychologically bruised, timid, and subdued social peer.

Barrio youngsters tend to be more subdued among whites, either because they know the whites don't like them, the strangeness of the social setting, or because they might have learned at home not to speak unless they are spoken to first. However, withdrawal behavior most probably is conditioned inertia. In effect, the consequence of normative ideals and reference group undermining any subsequent retardation in biosocial maturation they might have already experienced. Brown student inertia is, nonetheless, an undeniable expression of resistance and acquired inferiority. These schoolchildren appear timid and in a psychological state of withdrawal; doubtless, the result of constant frustration and accumulated anger.[31]

---

30. "Stranger in One's Land," *U.S. Commission on Civil Rights Clearinghouse Publication No. 19;* May 1970, pp. 23–29. This report represented one of the most incisive researched studies on Chicanos at the height of the Chicano movement in the 1970s.

31. Some of this anger and rage is often vented on the school structures and property. Vandalism is an immediate and unmistakable hostile expression directed at the school by frustrated and angry students.

That the intermediate school experience is a most highly critical period in the educational life of Chicanos is beyond academic debate. What educators presently know and understand of this level of instruction points to a juncture wherein most brown students pragmatically establish the psychological equilibrium "to make it," retaining a semblance of self-dignity, or in the face of continuing and overwhelming emotional odds, drop out.

WHITE MIDDLE-CLASS STANDARDS

Social scientists, in the past as well as in the present, have found that the best adjusted students (at least outwardly) are those from upper-class white, or non-white, but Anglo-integrated middle class backgrounds. But even with this head start, student adaptability to school life, at all levels of instruction, is largely dependent on the school's social curriculum. Fundamentally speaking, these students enter a "friendly" system that mirrors both their core value systems and social reference group with which they can identify, and which they firmly believe is their very own.

Also, since students are taught and socialized to believe the American credo that wealth is synonymous with intelligence, and that poverty is connected with failure, "Mexican" images become increasingly more negative in junior high school. Conversely, the self-esteem, image, and status of middle-class whites are appreciably enhanced.

The indifferent role teachers play here is another justifiable bone of contention among Chicano students. If judged on their role as substitute parents, teachers often fail because they are irresponsible, insensitive, and outright negligent by failing to correct the callous and untactful social behavior of white students toward brown students. Lamentably, unkind remarks and the denigration of "Mexican students" is sometimes overtly contributed to by the teachers themselves. Inasmuch as most teachers are products of the same middle-class environment and ethos as are most of their white students, considerable insensitivity pervades the social ambience.[32]

It is a truism the monocultural middle-class secular humanist core values and normative ideals of Anglo culture counter many of those held by Chicanos. Although cross-cultural values translation is possi-

---

32. *Teachers and Students*, p. 33.

ble, it is not a focal part of the social curriculum. Thus, brown Americans reared in barrios are at best superficially socialized to the dominant culture after ten years of public school instruction, and in the culture of alienation and denial as minorities. Since most Chicanos lack a personal experience or understanding of American secularism, marginal brown student products are caught in an endless state of apprehension and anxiety, by substituting white Anglo student patterns of behavior, and by imitating white Anglos. Ignored and overlooked are the Chicano student's *gente decente* values; values that are the equivalent of Anglo middle-class cultural ones.

Be that as it may, regardless of the intensity and persistence of a brown pupil's attempts at mimicking Anglo behavior patterns, his cultural naivete is usually manifest in social awkwardness and insecurity as new learning situations with whites arise. Moreover, white Anglo peer ridicule, amusement, and punishing criticism contributes to the frustration and anxiety. In short, a Chicano is entrapped in a social condition that accelerates an utter lack of originality that is self-denigrating and socially disintegrating. In effect, it deepens the desire and persistence to be more correctly and properly Anglo-like; and, a coincidental shame of being a Chicano or a Mexican is enhanced. The positive *Amor sui* (love of self) is lost in their developing Anglomania and culture of denial.

Middle-class white children are socialized and impelled by their parents, peers, teachers, and their social environment to believe in themselves, in success, and in intellectual achievement. In school this behavior is showcased by competitively earning good grades and high scores on examinations. In concert with this conviction, testing and tracking of students is considered a serious matter by most middle-class whites. To suggest that it is important to the general school community is superfluous.

Educators collectively concur that barrio pupils generally score lower than Anglos on English language middle-class oriented verbal-type tests. Given the problems of biosocial maturation retardation, with its consequent reduction of correct social skills and communication, and the useless individualistic idiom acquired by many brown American youngsters, that Spanish surname students tend to score lower on tests is not particularly surprising. Some materials are, in effect, structured to the disadvantage of Chicano students who are tested without compensation for their bicultural and bilingual background. Yet, despite being fully aware of this unfair standard of measurement, no significant corrective innovation has been forthcoming to ameliorate the academic and psychologically debilitating process.

A number of states continue to test youngsters in their initial year of junior high school, dismissing the ethnic or linguistic differentiation of brown pupils. Yet, the negative social implications on campus affected by unimaginative testing and tracking are at least threefold. First, the eventual low test scores reinforce the Chicano's socialized self-concept of lower mental capability. Second, the otherwise meaningless test scores are used by teachers and counselors to rank brown Americans as mentally inferior; a condition that reinforces their belief that brown pupils are innately inferior to whites. And finally, the fixed idea that Chicanos are uneducable and stupid is nourished.

UNITED STATES HISTORY AND BROWN AMERICANISM

A well-established and notably underplayed cause which advances negative Mexican images and stereotypes, and which directly and indirectly adversely affects Chicanos, is the presentation of United States history. Southwestern United States history continues to be extremely chauvinistic at all levels of instruction. During a period in their lives when young people keenly identify with hero images, the Chicano's ego-strength is constantly bombarded and disparaged by historical fantasy and distortion. Given the unique historical contact between Mexico and the United States, persons of Mexican descent are more susceptible to the biased American history syndrome.

It suffices to say most teachers have been influenced by the historical philosophy and fantasies of Frederick Jackson Turner, Justin H. Smith, Ray Allen Billington, Odie Faulk, and other nationalistic historians. So long as the texts and materials continue to present only slanted and biased accounts, and teachers continue to personalize American history by excluding colored Americans with the pronouns "we" and "they," the historical image of the Mexican American in United States history will remain unknown and unappreciated.

Impressionable young minds read of the acquisition of the Southwest by industrious, hardworking, progressive, Christian, Anglo-Americans from lazy, happy-go-lucky, papists, idolatrous Mexicans.[33] Even

---

33. See B. C. Orozco's, *Republican Protestantism in Aztlan,* (Glendale, CA, Petereins Press, 1980), passim, 79–95.

the remarkable mission systems founded in the now United States Southwest by Spanish and Mexican missionaries and frontiersmen are disparaged as institutions for Indian abuse and enslavement. Conversely, the white American is formed in the fantastic tradition of the heroic Beowulf, devoid of human shortcomings. While the westward movement is narrated as a providential mission effected by the "elect people" of Jehovah,[34] never mind the genocide campaign against the Indians and the many evils perpetrated on the Hispano Mexicans.

Chicano students endure unimaginable emotional distress on reading descriptions of Mexicans as treacherous and cowardly in the American conspired and supported Texas rebellion of 1836, and the American invasion of Mexico. Adherence to historical fantasy or distortion, and depiction of Mexicans as cowardly and anti-American breeds hatred and breaks adolescent friendships between white and brown students. White students learn contempt for Mexicans on reading slanted accounts of the war with Mexico. Contrary to the facts, the conflict is portrayed as having been an inexpensive and easy war. The invasion of Mexico was an expensive venture in terms of lives lost and the cost of the war for the period.[35] It was also the country's first war of conquest, a fact which rankles righteous sensibilities to this day.[36]

It would hearten Chicano pupils to learn their antecedents heroically defended their country at the fortress of the Alamo in Texas, and, against the invaders from the United States at the battles of Buena Vista, Padierna, San Pascual, Dominguez Hills, and Churubusco. As one historian put it, "Studied impartially [those battles] assume epic proportions comparable to many of the most celebrated major actions of the nineteenth century."[37] A potent and laudable tribute to the Mexican cause in view of the fierce fighting that took place during the Napoleonic wars and the American Civil War.

---

34. Americanist historians knowingly delude American readers with slanted historical accounts of United States westward movement history. See Orozco, *Ibid.*, pp. 79–85 and Philip W. Powell, *Tree of Hate: Propaganda and Prejudices Affecting United States Relations with the Hispanic World* (New York and London: Basic Books, Inc., Publishers, 1971), pp. 117–127.

35. The great California gold rush and the sobering Civil War that followed the Mexican American War overshadowed the cost and tragedy of the latter war.

36. This fact remains a sensitive historical point generally ignored by Americanist and nationalist historians.

37. *The Mexican Soldier* (Mexico: Nieto-Brown-Hefter, 1958), pp. 77–78. See also the diaries of generals Robert E. Lee and U. S. Grant on their Mexican War impressions.

Anglo-American historiography is rooted in British letters and unimaginable fantasy. A cursory examination of American southwestern history reveals an incredible analogy to the mythical English events and personality of Beowulf, the idealized dragon-killer. The tale of the "defeat" and destruction of the Spanish Armada which was no actual defeat at all is part of this fantastic scenario. This imaginary literary genre was refined in sketching the Anglo-American frontier and the westward march to the Pacific.[38]

For example, the serious student of Western Americana is often befuddled by the difficult task of discerning whether Sam Houston or Davy Crockett was the king of the "teller of tales." Since it was in Texas where some of the tallest tales originated, and since we are told Sam Houston's personal touch enhanced Texas tradition, then we can conjecture that he ranked with Crockett. We should not overlook the fact that Crockett died in Texas, "fighting like a tiger," or so tradition says.[39] In the epic of the winning of the American West Mexican frontiersmen are presented in folklore as quaint, greasy, cowardly peons although many had an ancestry of frontier fighting that predated the landing of the Mayflower. Incredibly, even Mexican outlaws are ranked below white American outlaws.

In sixteenth century English letters, piracy under the direction of Queen Elizabeth was England's feeble challenge to the might of Catholic Spain. In this fantasy heritage the Spanish are depicted as the "bad guys" although in historical truth it was the English buccaneers who were the criminals. The Anglo-American ethos includes these and other English traditions, but it fashioned its own peculiar new twist. Mexicans and Chicanos have emerged as uniformly "Spanish and, subsequently, as the perpetual enemies of English-speaking peoples."[40]

---

38. Professor Powell wrote extensively on this genre. See Powell, *Tree of Hate, passim*, pp. 39–46; See also Cecil Robinson *With The Ears of Strangers: The Mexican in American Literature*, (Tucson: The University of Arizona Press, 1969), pp. 31–66; and, E. C. Orozco, *Republican Protestantism in Aztlan*, pp. 79–104.

39. Extensive research by Walter Lord and others indicates he did not "die like a tiger." See Walter Lord, "Myths and Realities of the Alamo," *American West*, May, Vol. I, 1968.

40. Indeed, Oliver Cromwell popularized the idea that the Spanish were the "natural enemies of Englishmen." More importantly, however, is the English-speaking American citizen's inability and willingness to distinguish between Spaniards and Mexicans or Chicanos and Mexicans, when it is not politically convenient. See Philip Wayne Powell, *Tree of Hate*, p. 118.

Professor Philip Wayne Powell succinctly outlined the hostile legacy predating the Mexico-United States clash in the Southwest in the nineteenth century:

> In the intellectual modes that crystallized in the United States during the nineteenth century and often extended to the present, there are several main lines in which popularization of hispanophobic biases is clearly seen. Some of our frontier clashes were still, irritatingly, with the Spanish (or Mexicans), and in the Texan-Mexican struggle and then in our war with Mexico, we transferred some of our ingrained antipathy toward Catholic Spain in her American heirs . . . This abrasive proximity to persons of Spanish speech, especially a darker-hued Mexican encouraged our faith in Nordic superiority. It was a small step, really, from "Remember the Armada" to "Remember the Alamo."[41]

In this context it is not particularly difficult to comprehend why young minds can find little pride in being Spanish surnamed, Spanish speaking, or of Mexican ancestry. The social condition can be made so tense that as Chicanos grow in their defensiveness and imposed shame in being of Mexican ancestry, white students mature in the glorification of their designated role of superiority over Mexicans and Chicanos. The social condition festers and offends.

Even the few major brown heroes who merit public attention and distinction are commonly disclaimed as Chicanos by the dishonest inference they are of mixed ancestry (part Anglo or Spanish), rather than of Mexican or of Chicano origin. The time-honored practice of isolating or ignoring brown heroes is effective. A classic example of this practice is the heroics of brown American servicemen who served in World War II, Korea, and Vietnam. The valor and military accomplishments of many brown Americans is one of the greatest military secrets in United States history—over twenty Congressional Medal of Honor winners![42]

The uninhibited popular practice of repudiating Chicano success by attributing to a white person the merit for that success is another

---

41. *Ibid,* Powell, *Tree of Hate,* p. 118.

42. See Raul Morin, *Among the Valiant: Mexican Americans in World War II and Korea* (Alhambra, California, Borden Publishing Co., 1966).

mechanism effectively applied to infer that brown persons are incapable of achieving success on their own merit. To be credible the Chicano personality either has to become totally psychologically American, or a white person has to somehow show him the secret or direction to success.

A strong counter argument can be made with the thousands of recently resettled adult Asian immigrants. Many without any past business experience whatsoever have materially succeeded in the southwestern United States. Moreover, many have achieved this great success without having had to relinquish ethnic or racial ties. Unencumbered by psychological racial disorders, such as feelings of racial or cultural inferiority, their personal efforts and energy have been confined to industry, progress, and economic prosperity.

However, manifestations of psychological disorder similar to those of other American colored minorities are becoming more evident among their school-aged children. As the schools enforce minority inferiority self-images and substitute patterns of behavior among their school-aged children, the latter are beginning to mirror a behavior very similar to that of disaffected Chicanos. Frustration, cultural alienation, anger, and self-hate is driving many to hostile gang activity.

CHAPTER 6

Early Adolescent Years:

Brown American Authority Models

*G*iven that American culture is structured to divide minority alliances tied by race or culture, it is not all too surprising to recognize that the employment of brown American teachers does not always necessarily benefit Chicano students. Many Mexican American teachers are, in fact, quite antipathetic to Mexicanism, or they possess uncompromising hostile brown phobic attitudes; sentiments that are often counter-productive in Chicano pupil encounters with these authority model figures.

Yet, in all fairness to most brown teachers, it should be stressed that any preference to be identified as Spanish, and any reticence on their part to work with brown pupils, is most irrefutably rooted in their own personal systematic psychological processing to deculturate, followed by assimilation. As youngsters they were not immune to the intense social mandates and pressures brought upon them to renounce their brown race and Hispano Mexican heritage. Besides, they assuredly gained a semblance of stature or status through accommodation and by the objectifying of Mexicans as inferior to whites. In effect, their Anglo-like point of reference, self-centeredness, and affectation is what defeats or counters whatever positive influence their presence might otherwise have to inspire brown barrio students to emulate them. Brown American teachers' brown phobia is cultivated by the very same school social curriculum of which they have become an institutionalized cog. Socially and culturally they personify the disintegrated anti-Mexican living examples of the schools' psychological apartheid process described above.

In view of the culture of denial processing, it surely is not too alarming that relatively few aspiring brown Anglo teachers are prepared or inclined to teach in predominantly "Chicano schools."[43] In this connection, behavioral patterns of insecurity among aspiring brown Anglo administrators and teachers are indisputable, deep-rooted manifestations of feelings of inferiority and antipathy toward their former reference group's normative ideals.[44]

An analogy between a brown teacher who aspires to be Anglo-like and a psychologically insecure aspirant brown policeman is apropos. Particularly if the latter believes he must prove to his white comrades that he is more concerned than they about "cleaning up the barrio streets of crime." To justify his one-man crusade in the barrios in order to prove his point, his treatment of Chicanos, subsequently, may be harsher of tone and manner since he has a fixation that in this manner he will gain the approbation of his fellow white officers. His unreasonable and confused point of reference will always transcend normal procedures of law enforcement.

Moved by powerful hidden emotional needs and personal instinct, the brown policeman assumes a self-ascribed role to correct the presumed non-conforming and embarrassing behavior of belligerent American-like Chicanos. Since in fact, as a policeman he may be of the frank opinion that he has "made it," he is intolerant of excuses even among the marginally socially deviant. If they have failed "to make it," it is the result of laziness, or a lack of ambition. In short, he lives by the popular Anglo adage that failure among minorities is due to their own lack of personal effort.

Countless marginal and culturally alienated brown Americans have accepted this social Darwinist and supremacist rationale without question. Because it requires a simple preconditioning of the mind, predicated on the WASP principle that it is best to conform to gain the approbation of the majority than to resist and remain free. In other

---

43. *Teachers and Students*, pp. 27–28.

44. Countless brown Americans are in positions of authority in the school districts where brown American children attend in large numbers, but for the most part they are content to leave well enough alone.

words, emasculation of the human spirit and coalescing with evil (i.e., ignorance) is considered a fair exchange for a little social recognition and peripheral acceptance by the white majority. No more convincing proof can be adduced to underline the foolishness of this false philosophy than the exceedingly tragic results the schools have perpetrated on the brown American community.

This state of affairs points to the growing number of alienated and antipathetic brown Anglo teachers and administrators brown pupils are encountering. It is making little positive impact.[45] It could hardly be otherwise given the latter's estimation, that association with Mexicans reflects poor American social etiquette. For among white Americans the general conviction is that "Mexicans" should mix and blend, to demonstrate to others they have broken the contemptible "Mexican" bond. No one has ever suggested that whites should break their alliances in order to blend with the darker races. This mode of thinking ultimately is mere fantasy because the brown American has not been afforded the opportunity to choose to be his own man.

Another foolish notion propagated by white Americans that has thrived, is the belief among all Americans that colored persons must be many times better than whites just to be the latter's equal. It is an effective time-honored colonialist mechanism. Ergo, the aspiring brown Anglo's preference to associate and hob-nob with the traditional models of authority and power, the white Anglos. And by extension, it serves to support the latter's stance of inequality, injustice, and legacy of hate against the Hispano Mexicans.

In the classroom and in other competitive situations between whites and brown students, research studies show the latter are at a marked disadvantage to whites. The belief among Americans that whites are naturally superior to the colored races is a foregone conclusion. To a predominant number of teachers (this is prevalent on the college and university level as well), Chicanos must prove themselves to be many times better than whites just to rate an equal or superior grade.

In this regard, teachers have been known to express surprise when a brown pupil masters a given subject or problem with relative ease. Conversely, failure among brown students elicits little teacher response because failure among them is generally expected. Consequently,

---

45. The number is greater but proportionately Spanish surnamed teachers make up 3% of all teachers while whites constitute 68%. See Sed *National Education Association, NEA Survey,* July, 1992.

demanding and exacting superior academic performance from brown pupils results in a declining number of superior Spanish surname students, and a disproportionately larger number of frustrated ones.

The seriousness of this obviously unfair and undemocratic measurement can be gauged by the negative psychological affecting it has on Chicanos. It forces brown pupils to become defensive and gravely compounds their already nascent conditioned feelings of inferiority. Ethnocentric, meaning Eurocentric, oriented textbooks, prejudiced teachers, counselors, administrators, and alienated brown Anglos multiply and reinforce this drift of perverted consciousness. Incredibly, the primary school serves as the substructure for the development of this mental framework. Subsequent junior and senior high school training builds on that base.

With all this, it is, nonetheless, revealing to many teachers who, when they go against the popularly accepted teacher grain, their professional credibility is questioned. A secondary Chicano school teacher, for example, who was fair and egalitarian in his measurement of students enrolled in his Spanish classes, surprised many teachers and students on campus when at year's end four of the five foreign language awards forthcoming from his classes went to brown Spanish surnamed pupils. This evident fair recognition of performance was criticized by teachers and students who presumed the "Mexicans" already knew the language, and, in effect, had an advantage over white students. Now, using that logic, since English is the native idiom of most white Americans, should they be excluded from English awards in which Chicanos are also in competition?[46]

A lack of multicultural sensitive teachers and administrators of any race is a lamentable problem in itself. But doesn't common sense dictate that a total absence of sensitized brown teachers and administrators only serves to reinforce Mexican and Chicano inferiority? Particularly, when the authority-leadership-intelligent-figure-model forever remains white. Inasmuch as Chicano pupils rarely see real brown authority figures in school or in real societal experiences, it nurtures another expectation cue. That is, that when a Chicano authority-leadership figure is encountered, he is expected to be Anglo-like (the symbol of success and

---

46. The teacher is the author of this book. Three of the four brown students who received recognition for academic performance have since achieved the following: one is an editorial-journalist for a major Los Angeles newspaper. A second did graduate studies in linguistics at UCLA, and the third earned his law degree and is practicing law.

authority) because he will be judged by the former, as a neo-Chicano activist once aptly worded it, "through-gringo colored eyes."

Experience has taught many Mexican American administrators and teachers that, in general, they are not regarded to be as capable in their disciplines or positions as whites; also, often by members of the Spanish surnamed brown group itself. The brown American authority figure finds itself in the unfortunate and invidious focal position of having to prove itself to both whites and browns as an Anglo, and not as a Chicano! How, then, can they ever believe they have any rational grounds for proving themselves as Latinos or Hispanics? The plot thickens.

A DESIGN FOR INFERIORITY REINFORCEMENT

Subtle practices to condition and motivate Chicanos to belittle themselves and members of their group do not dissipate simply because someone suggests they no longer exist. Credible and respected federal Civil Rights Commission studies have documented white Anglo teacher practices in which Mexican American students were systematically excluded from classroom participation.[47] Classroom practices of this nature further advance sentiments among students that whites are superior and more intelligent than Chicanos. In effect, these government studies are but a transparent exposé of the differential and aversive conditioning methodology used in the schools, in concert with the ugly psychology leveled on brown students by the schools' social curriculum of white race glorification and superiority.

The focus on college preparation and tracking by many schools further limits contact between academic subject teachers and Chicanos. Brown American students tend to experience disproportionate contact with less quality teaching. That condition, in actuality, is consistent with all lower academic caliber students. Moreover, non-academic teachers in general tend to be less sensitized and prepared to teach minority youngsters. This means, of course, that the wood shop or metal shop teacher are expected to be more readily disposed to react negatively, and more harshly, to Chicano psychology and horseplay as documentation demonstrates.

Conversely, the academically prepared teacher may demonstrate coarse smugness because of the academically advanced level of students

47. *Teachers and Students*, p. 28.

he or she has been assigned to teach. Since "Mexicans" normally are not tracked into these classes in large numbers, frowning on those few who do enroll in their classes is clearly a negative teacher response. A teacher's institutionalized prejudices and myopia regarding a brown student's presumed mental incapacity in a given classroom situation takes care of the rest.

Thus, those teachers who expect less performance from Chicanos may inadvertently abuse and coerce "Mexican" students for intended greater effort. In review, a teaching practice which many educational psychologists theorize cultivates mental blocks. Because of the differential treatment they receive, in concert with these practices, Chicanos are gradually overwhelmed in their quest to earn academic, athletic, or social recognition on their own merit like other students. Incredible as it may initially sound, inferiority reinforcement is evident even in situations where brown pupils constitute the majority of the student or school community.

The monocultural social and academic curriculum is common throughout the country's public schools. Cognizant of the schools' status quo format can make school busing for racial integration purposes all the more unreasonable and foolish. Multicultural and racial diversity classroom instruction can achieve far greater results and benefits for the greater number, as opposed to mandatory busing. The latter action serves to antagonize otherwise ethnically neutral democratic centered parents who, by this practice, lose some of the control they possess in educating their children. Taking or reducing one group's freedom to pacify and appease another serves injustice.

A SAD COMMENTARY

In Los Angeles, California, approximately six out of every ten Chicano pupils drop out of junior and senior high school. In Texas, the combined dropout rate is reported to be as high as seventy percent in some regions.[48] The causes for the astronomical dropout rate among brown

---

48. *The American Commission on Civil Rights* compiled a 269-page report in 1974 in which it categorically surmised from it's five-year study that the "public school system not only ignores the educational needs of Chicano students but also suppresses their culture and stifles their hopes and ambitions." See "Toward Quality Education for Mexicans." The report offered fifty-one specific recommendations for change and improvement. Most were ignored. So in 1990 when the National Council of La Reza reported that "Hispanics were the most poorly educated," they were not exaggerating. See *Los Angeles Daily News,* July 1, 1990.

Spanish surname students are well-known, and documentation on the causes is available in research projects done by doctoral candidates and educational agencies dating to the 1920s.

Frankly speaking, after these many years, and the accumulation of research done on the subject, it is difficult to reconcile the absence of deed with the urgency of the need because so few positive long-term corrective measures have ever been implemented. To the knowledgeable, the lame excuse that further research is needed to better understand the problem falls on deaf ears.[49] The inevitable conclusion is that the schools are knee-deep in anti-Mexican bigotry.

By the ninth grade, both white and brown American pupils in many schools have settled their differences; that is, each goes his own way making the separation complete. A ninth-grader may no longer resort to calling a Chicano a "beaner" or a "wetback," preferring to openly ignore or shun him. Barrio Chicanos, conversely, may refer to whites as *"gabachos"* or "paddies" and gradually restrict their social contacts to exclusively Chicano ones. Hence, most Chicanos are psychologically and socially separated from Anglos by an unchanging narrow social curriculum by the time they leave junior high school.

Yet with all this, the inner workings, the progression to Chicano social disintegration, alienation, and an acquired sense of inferiority are difficult to assess and to fathom. A victimized personality's own testimony is doubtless the best vehicle by which to better comprehend the depth of helplessness and sense of rejection. Of the succeeding narratives, the first comments are those of a Mexican American woman who was in her late thirties at the time she expressed them:

> Until I went to school at the age of 4 I was simply Rosita. Then I entered school, and I discovered, first of all, I was Mexican—never American. This despite being a citizen of the United States. I accepted this label without question along with being treated differently than my fellow Anglo students . . .

> By the time I reached junior high school, I had crawled into a shell, I tended to diagnose my trouble as identity dilemma. I have always loved the English language and the United States. This is my home. The only country I know. My insides do not see color; they only know and feel American.

---

49. The American Council of Education—See p. 83 m85.

Of course, my mother imbued me with the rich heritage of Mexico, the land of my parents and grandparents. I have always been proud of my Mexican heritage, but I am equally proud of my country's heritage.

I am as at home with hamburgers and french fries as I am with *chorizo* and *huevos*. Bread and tortillas, English and Spanish, Abraham Lincoln and Benito Juarez—all of these things are me.

But they were not acceptable. One incident particularly sticks out in my memory. I was 12 years old and just starting out in the seventh grade, the only Chicana in the class. The teacher singled me out to stand up after we had just filled out some information forms. In the space where it said "race" I had in all innocence written "American."

"No," said the teacher in an annoyed tone of voice, "you have to write 'Mexican.'"

My face burned red because she made me feel as if I had committed a terrible wrong, but for the first time in my life I fought back. I wanted desperately to be like everyone else. "No, I'm American," I said. Every Anglo in the room was staring at me as she insisted, "No, your race is Mexican."

"I was born here in Pasadena. I'm American." I persisted, almost crying. Finally, angrily, she took the card and wrote in "Mexican" herself.

It was soon after that I dropped out of school. So Mexican was made a dirty word for me.[50]

A thirteen-year-old Mexican American girl, "attractive, articulate, an honor student, member of the band, outstanding in girls' athletics, popular among her peers and fellow students, and admired by her teachers," and evidently without any visible problem wrote the incredibly candid narrative below in response to an assignment in class:

To begin with, I am a Mexican. That sentence has a scent of bitterness as it is written. I feel that if it weren't for my nationality I would accomplish more. My being a Mexican has brought about my lack of initiative. No matter what I attempt to do, my dark skin always makes me feel that I will fail. Another thing that "gripes" me is that I am such a coward. I absolutely will not fight for something even if I know

---

50. In author's files, May 11, 1973.

I'm right. I do not have the vocabulary that it would take to express myself strongly enough. Many people, including most of my teachers, have tried to tell me I'm a leader. Well, I know better. Just because I may get better grades than most of my fellow Mexicans doesn't mean a thing. I could no more get an original idea in my head than be President of the United States. I don't know how to think for myself.

I want to go to college, sure, but what do I want to be? Even worse, where do I want to go? These questions are only a few that trouble me. I'd like to prove to my parents that I can do something. Just because I don't have gumption to go out and get a job doesn't mean that I can't become something they'll be proud of. But if I find that I can't bring myself to go to college, I'll get married and they'll still get rid of me.

After reading this, you'll probably be surprised. This is the way I feel about myself, and nobody can change me. Believe me, many have tried and have failed. If God wants me to reach all my goals, I will. No parents, teachers, or priests will change the course that my life is to follow. Don't try.[51]

In the past and in the immediate present, little innovation has been forthcoming from teacher and educator groups to correct, on any scale, some of the major problems that nurture mental blocks to learning, negativism, and the development of inferior self-images among Chicanos. This decades-long inaction leads to two logical conclusions: First, too few teachers and school administrators consider it a sufficiently grave matter to warrant change. Second, Chicano students have been written off and few persons honestly care to see them succeed educationally. Thus, further academic debate on the issue is fruitless because the systematic cultivation of the potential Chicano sit-in and drop out is something most educators reflexively have left for someone else to resolve—obviously by the Chicanos themselves.

All this means, of course, that the negative assertions made by educators such as "those Mexicans don't want to be Americans," or "those Mexicans don't want to learn" are dishonest and malicious. Doubtless, the vile commentary is directed to distort and conceal an

51. *The Invisible Minority.* Report of the NEA–Tucson Survey on Teaching of Spanish to the Spanish Speaking. Washington DC: Department of Rural Education, National Education Association, 1966, p. 3.

obviously narrow curriculum, poor teaching methodology, aversive conditioning, and counseling deficiencies characteristic of the public schools in the Southwest.

The social condition directives persist in their uncompromising expectation that Chicanos acquire substitute patterns of behavior; that they learn to behave like middle-class white Anglos. All this in order to be at least peripherally accepted as worthy persons. Moreover, they should learn to speak impeccable English and to speak out if they wish to be treated decently. If they are not accorded correct treatment and they remain silent, then, that is their problem.[52]

For all that has been debated, it is vital to stress that as brown students progress from primary school to senior high school, rejection of their Mexican ancestry is coincidentally chronologically progressive. While aspiring brown Anglos, and the more Anglo-like brown students, arguably might be more acceptable to whites, at least on the surface, in the main all brown students are stereotyped as Mexicans by the majority group usually because of their colored skin and Spanish surname. Given the framework of the educational experience described above, the Chicano student, unlike the more Anglo-like brown students, shrinks socially, and psychologically withdraws under the weight of the same conditioning and negative social cues.

Although many brown pupils become potential dropouts by the completion of middle school, the more resilient usually do not prematurely depart until they experience their baptism by fire in senior high school. Happily for many students, early adolescence is fairly spent out by the end of the intermediate school years. But, before they are academically prepared and socialized, a disproportionate number of students never do adjust.

Nonetheless, upon terminating middle school, white youngsters look forward to a different school setting with widened freedom. Chicanos anxiously wait, somewhat skeptically, for a better and more egalitarian and positive social situation. Some, incredibly, still see a light at the end of the tunnel they are caught in. Unfortunately for the students, the schools form tunnels for colored and minority youngsters, not bridges. A youngster cannot jump off a tunnel like he might be able to if he were on a bridge.

---

52. When Chicanos do speak out in protest like other Americans they are accused of being anti-American, and ridiculously even un-American. See Chapters 7 and 8.

CHAPTER 7

The Later Adolescent Years:

Beyond the Crossroads

*D*ropout rates for nearly two generations of Mexican Americans have been notably high in senior high school. Often cited as primary causes for pre-World War II brown students dropping out of school were language handicaps, poverty, family indifference, and racism. However, in synthesizing the record from glimpses of the past, a little more precise scenario emerges. Unfortunately, social scientists have little knowledge of Mexican American demographics predating the Mexican immigrant surge north of the border from 1910 to 1940.

Nevertheless, in respect to both brown Americans and Mexican immigrants Jay Stowell, a Protestant proselytizer working among the Mexicans, wrote:

> All of these Border towns have recently received a fresh influx of Mexicans. From these Mexican homes come throngs of bright boys and girls with all the good wishes of fond parents who want their children to enjoy all of the advantages which American children have. In an overwhelming proportion of cases, however, their hopes are doomed to disappointments. The entire trail of the public school in the Southwest is strewn with the blasted hopes of Mexican boys and girls. By the time high school is reached there are few left, and of those who complete a high school course the number is small indeed. The

proportion varies from city to city, but in general it is always small and sometimes almost negligible.[53]

Social scientists observed that most Mexican immigrant families migrated north from regions in Mexico where an education tradition was not an established way of life among the masses. The record is clear, the immigrants were miserably poor and generally illiterate peons and *campesinos*. Moreover, given the negative status of Mexicans in the American ethos, compounded by their general impoverishment and subsequent demoralization in the United States, it was expected that little headway would have been made. Additionally, Mexican attempts to develop a positive education tradition were successfully obstructed. Given all this, a negative attitude toward American education by the immigrants would have been expected.

Yet, the evidence available to us documents precisely the opposite kind of response scenario. For example, Reverend Robert McLean, a Methodist minister, wrote in 1928:

> In the Los Angeles school district, there are at present time more than thirty-two thousand Mexican children. While the language disability prevails, or where there has been retardation due to migration, they are placed in "opportunity rooms" where circumstantial disability is not in evidence, they seem to keep pace in their classes with our own children. In the Ramona School in Los Angeles a teacher was given seventy-five Mexican children as "opportunity" pupils. So diligent were they in their application, and so successful in their studies, that in seven months they had made the same progress which the ordinary child makes in fourteen months. Perhaps in some degree their ability is enhanced by their mental hunger. As Professor Harry M. Shafer of the Los Angeles School Board says: "So great is the hunger of these Mexican children, and so great is the zeal of their parents for them, that they are liable to outdistance our own boys and girls in their school work. So often American parents insist that they do not want their children to avail themselves of certain privileges which are offered, while the Mexican parent frankly declares that he wants his child to have advantage of every opportunity which is provided.[54]

---

53. Jay S. Stowell, *The Near Side of the Mexican Question* (New York: George H. Doran Company, 1921), p. 90.

54. Robert McLean, *That Mexican* (New York: Fleming H. Revell Co., 1928), pp. 24–25.

Reverend Stowell described the education of Mexicans in San Antonio, Texas, as follows:

They will deny themselves the bare necessities of life that their children may be supplied school books. Nothing that will benefit or uplift is withheld. Not only do they think of their own, but find in nearly every family some orphan who receives the same consideration as their own child. As is often the case with foreigners, you never hear of a Mexican taking his child out of school for the reason that it has had opportunity enough and must go to work to repay parents. The children are only taken out of school for sheer need, or because they are oversized and ashamed to be with smaller ones, or because of race prejudice against them being so strong that they forego an education rather than submit to the conditions imposed.[55]

Professor B. O. Schrieke observed in 1936 that in most rural Texas schools neither pretense nor effort was made:

. . . to enforce on Mexican children the state compulsory attendance law. For those Mexicans who do attend school, the facilities in most aspects are obviously below those provided for American children. This is true with respect to buildings, equipment, and room space per pupil frequently with respect to the salary scale of teachers; and frequently, though by no means always, with respect to the grades offered in the "Mexican" school; either another grade (without adequate equipment) is added to the instructional duties of the teachers in the Mexican school, or pupils just end their schooling, or go elsewhere for it.[56]

Una Lawrence, another Protestant proselytizer, shed additional light on the rigid social barriers in force against "Mexicans" who aspired to advance academically. Lawrence wrote:

This is a Mexican community of superior type. There are several minor businesses owned and operated by Mexicans. But the Mexican community is entirely separate from the American. No Mexican is permitted to own property in the American community. No Mexican boy or girl has ever entered the high school of this town; though the

---

55. Stowell, *The Near Side of the Mexican Question*, p. 91.

56. B. O. Schrieke, *Alien Americans: A Study of Race Relations* (New York: The Viking Press, 1936), p. 50.

Mexicans have always lived in this town. They are not the migrant labor type.

Last year the son of a Mexican business man was ready for high school, having finished grammar grade work by private teaching. Knowing public sentiment, the father sent him to a city 200 miles away rather than risk the ill-will and boycott his business might suffer if he applied for entrance to the high school in his own town.[57]

Consequently, attempts by Mexican immigrants and their descendants to develop an education tradition in the United States were iniquitously aborted at every turn. Prejudice, racial discrimination, and social custom were the indisputable principal barriers to an equal educational opportunity for brown students with Spanish surnames. In that era white Americans were not inclined to extend economic opportunity and social equality to "Mexicans." In fact, it is highly doubtful whether that attitude ever really changed.

THE ORIGINS OF A DROPOUT TRADITION

When examined and studied objectively, the treatment accorded Mexicans and Mexican Americans in the past can help us better understand the rationale behind a large proportion of the Chicano population being habituated to not attending school today, or striving for higher education goals. In the past, "Mexicans" were clearly made aware that a high school education was intended for white American youngsters only.

Unlike the Spanish colonial period of Mexico they were not expected or encouraged to share in the breath of American culture. Brown youngsters who sought a high school education invariably suffered and endured many indignities; a wretched school social practice that contributed to their failure or premature school termination, in effect, as we previously examined, Mexican and Mexican American children were discouraged from pursuing educational goals beyond grade school. In short, they were encouraged to drop out of school because they were not wanted.

---

57. Una Lawrence, *Winning the Border* (Atlanta: Home Mission Board, Southern Baptist Convention, 1935), p. 74. All these observations were of the frank opinion that social custom did not favor permitting Mexicans being educated.

The major cornerstones on which the present-day dropout tradition of Mexican American youngsters was nurtured, were indeed calculated social exclusion and racial discrimination. But the more pervasive causes in recent times have been aversive conditioning and deculturation. In the urban Southwest a high percentage of school dropouts cluster in hostile gangs and become barrio social delinquents; which in turn gives rise to the not uniquely brown American urban *bato loco* (hoodlum) experience.[58]

The latter social problem was aggravated with compulsory school attendance in the years following World War II. While social disorientation and maladjustment is characteristically common among ethnic transitional types and marginal youth in American urban life, it surfaced for the first time among Mexican American youth during the *Pachuco zoot* suit episode in the 1940s.

Cruel deculturation, insensitive teachers, differential conditioning, and the aversive individualization of the personality are the primary causes for ravaged personalities and damaged spirits. This case scenario is most evident and most traumatic among those young persons who stem from traditional cultural backgrounds. To the gang culture knowledgeable, a notably defensive hostile demeanor, in concert with incoherent speech patterns, are irrefutable behavioral traits of differential negative conditioning, marginalism, and of the American secularization process. A person devoid of this understanding and acknowledgment can hardly be expected to come to grips with the actual causes that have made the scandalous dropout rate among brown students what it presently is.

Although in our times language incapacity among the greater majority of brown American youngsters is no longer a significant barrier to learning, the high dropout rate continues. Indeed, research done during the past two decades has categorically established that many brown American dropouts possess good, and often better than average English speaking and reading skills. But a deep-rooted antagonism toward school is also revealed, as well as a serious distaste for acquiescing to the school's subtle anti-Mexican social program.

This specific bared antagonistic and withdrawal behavior among these youngsters strongly suggests student attempts to control what

---

58. See Frederic M. Thrasher, *The Gang: A Study of 1,313 Gangs in Chicago* (Chicago: University of Chicago Press, 3rd ed., 1968), passim, pp. 21–62.

they wish to assimilate. Furthermore, this serious response marks a Chicano student inertia which is, in effect, a not too subtle form of resistance. Students generate this mild defensive response to counter the social program of humiliation directed at them.

Be that as it may, the vilification and social ostracism of "Mexicans" in both urban and rural areas persists as a way of life on school campuses. Unchanged, too, is the lower social positioning of the "Mexican-looking" brown American. Assuredly so long as the schools continue the social program that humiliates and degrades brown students of Mexican descent, these sentiments will persist. Southwestern American socialization is inclusive of an established and accepted regional bias that "Mexicans" are lower class, dirty, foreign, and anti-American. A mind-set and social condition initially impressed by violence, and later sustained by vile suppression.

Social custom guided by a racially generated popular ill will has fueled and sustained considerable sociological displacement in the brown American community. White American antagonistic sentiments have characteristically perpetuated the social isolation, and hence, the violent cycle of poverty of the Chicano population. In addition, unfair and discriminatory employment practices have spawned other problems which have, in a variety of ways, contributed to the Chicano's high dropout rate.

A LILY WHITE, MIDDLE-CLASS DOCTRINE

Accountability demands and any notably harsh allegation of wrongdoing by the country's public schools by Chicanos is rejected by white Americans, who not too often make little attempt to hide their disdain for "Mexicans" of any color or hue. They adamantly refuse to subscribe to any conclusion based on any given evidence that the schools spawn many of the social problems, which in turn taxes society's public service resources. Yet, for all their defensive rhetoric, the schools nonetheless cultivate more than anti-Mexicanism and social problems for Chicanos in particular and for society in general.

Education specialists have long been aware that the schools nurture socially deprived students, because most pupils are given little opportunity to socialize more democratically. Student campus politics, extracurricular activities, and campus leadership roles, for example, were in the past too often reserved for or tailored for middle-class white students. They still are in many schools. Rigid qualifications intended to directly or indirectly reject non-conformity and reward conformity, are established standards by which to weed out, or as some prefer, to standardize, lower class whites and minorities. This long-established anti-diversity social integration favoritism remains standard practice in many Southwestern schools in which Chicanos are the numerical majority.

Because of their ethnicity brown students are, therefore, systematically deprived of any hope of being somebody in the school social setting. Institutionalized social inequality and deprivation of any minority impacts all students negatively since vile attitudes held by any group toward another are incidentally and coincidentally impressed. A multicultural equality and diversity would ameliorate considerable resentment and racial antagonisms on campuses. Students have to be classroom-taught to respect these cultures. As a viable human learning experience presently folk dances and music are not enough unless it were done on a weekly basis.

Allegations echoed by educators that the schools also graduate ethnically deprived students are not totally unfounded. Most high school graduates, sound research reveals, possess little understanding of what it means to be Chicano, black, Jewish, or Asian in the United States. In fact, minority students also learn little that is substantively positive about Caucasian American character and American society. That it is rare for colored minorities to learn about their own particular group's contributions to the development of the United States is truly astonishing.[59]

This deficient and imbalanced curriculum is a time-honored learning condition school policy. Frankly, a perfunctory review points to existing policies that continue to be developed and guided by this elitist and narrow monocultural social custom. They are narrow and

---

59. A more potent hostility among the races can be found among high schoolers. Ignorance generates unpredictable and unexpected violence among them, although violence between black and brown students is more common than between minority and white students. Multiculturalism is feared by the white majority for a variety of reasons, the primary one being that it places all races on an equal footing. Whereas in the past ethnic "separatism" was favored by the white Establishment, the so-called minorities favor the meritorious inclusion of all Americans as co-equal in the American experience, and the exclusion of none. In actuality it is the road to racial tolerance, eventual racial harmony, and true equality.

supremacist because they represent antiquated trends that discourage a more comprehensive acknowledgment of the ethnic diversity of the United States. In all candor, it is superfluous to suggest that any practice of omission deprives most students of their individual potential to develop critically in reference to the ethnicity of America.

Moreover, it encourages and promotes a general callous ethnic insensitivity, and contributes to the social distance among school peers. These attitudes indisputably based on some perverted educational premise are cultivated through blatant rejection. How did that old saying go? "If you're white, you're alright, if you're black, stand back!, if you're brown, stick around." One has got to wonder, whatever happened to the Chinos, (i.e., Asians), in this great hierarchy. "No, no," retorted the petite Viet femme to the Chicano who told the Nahuatl "God and the Oven Creation of Mankind" story, that inferred God had perfected his creation with the making of the reddish-brown race; "God put some more dough into the oven," she added, "and wah-la He created the golden-brown Asian race. Then, He was done."[60]

At any rate, by calculated design of omission, elementary and high school students are deprived of their natural right to learn the more comprehensive colored minority heritage of America. Furthermore, colored (Asian, black, Chicano) students customarily complete their school experience shamefully unaware of the heritage of their own ethnicity as well as that of others. The void and absence of feelings of self-worth and a positive colored race self-awareness among Chicanos and blacks is fully nurtured here. More difficult to comprehend is that it marks a lamentable by-product of a school system totally unconcerned with the intolerable socio-psychological conflict, social misdirection, and wasted energy it continues to generate in the real world beyond the confines of the campus.

Preliminary tabulations from a 1973–1976 and a follow-up 1983–1986 Los Angeles, California, county-wide survey among brown American college and university students, sheds some light on the general ignorance of brown students regarding their own race and ethnicity (see Illustration on page 66). The Orozco Report also illustrates that brown American student knowledge of whites is no more profound than the latter's knowledge of Chicanos. This absolutely shameless

---

60. The irony today is that students are being sensitized by the schools to sexism and homophobia but nothing addresses racism and race identity.

chasm underscores the schools inadequate social curriculum and general lack of an ethnic diversity program.[61]

For example, to the question: "Which comes closest to your feeling for the term 'Anglo,'" the most profound term sixty and eighty-three percent, respectfully, of the brown respondents could connect with the label was "White Man!" Ironically, that response was not much superior to the normal white respondents' generic cognition of the brown American as a "Mexican." The latter point of reference is premised on the popular stereotypical assumption or notion that all Mexicans have brown skins and Spanish surnames.

In all sincerity, far more astonishing to the Chicano scholar is the lack of consensus among the vast majority of the brown respondents regarding their own biological identity. Since, in fact, they are never instructed or informed about their race in school, little foundation exists for these students to make a definitive and intelligent conclusion regarding the most fundamental characteristic of their own heritage. To the question, "To What Race Do You Believe Chicanos Belong?" remarkably, in the 1973–1976 tabulation only one-third of the respondents answered that a new classification is needed, compared to the 1983–1986 respondents' view of 43.6% (see Illustration on page 67). Still, that mental condition is not all that earth-shattering in view of the fact that most teachers, at all levels of instruction, are as equally confused and generally as ignorant regarding the Mexican's true racial background.

---

61. Twenty years following the height of the Chicano movement the Los Angeles City Schools approved Ethnic studies as elective courses set to begin in September 1991. It is not clear if they were actually included in the curriculum in 1991. See *Los Angeles Times,* September 11, 1990.

What race do you believe Chicanos belong to?

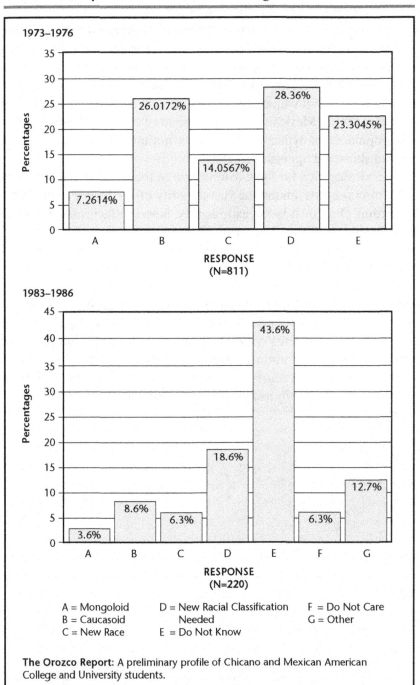

The Orozco Report: A preliminary profile of Chicano and Mexican American College and University students.

Which of the following comes closest to your feeling for the term Anglo?

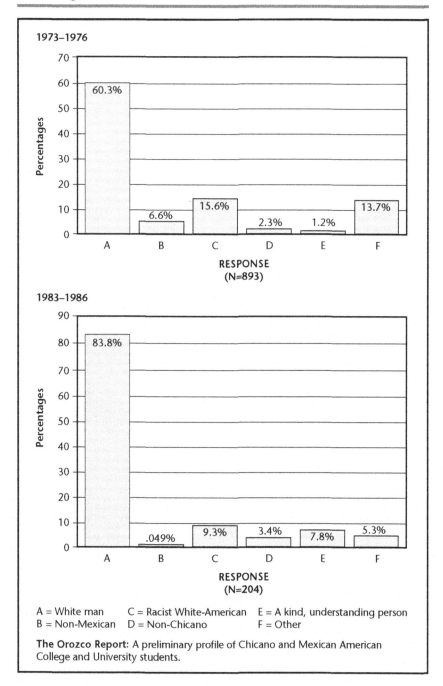

A = White man   C = Racist White-American   E = A kind, understanding person
B = Non-Mexican   D = Non-Chicano   F = Other

The Orozco Report: A preliminary profile of Chicano and Mexican American College and University students.

CHAPTER 8

The Timeless Philosophical Impasse:

Nature vs. God

*A*democratic society demands a literate and vocal body-politic. Written and oral self-expression are constitutional guarantees that are indispensable tools in a democratic republic. But, in spite of this presumably given natural right, American schools have not always presented the great majority of students with the best possible education. It is common knowledge to most educators that native white Americans are notoriously linguistically deficient in their parent idiom; but, this is a negative reflection of the public school system.

With this in mind it is strange that although the English language has never been a prerequisite for citizenship, monolingualism (i.e., total exclusion of other languages) has, nevertheless, been demanded of linguistically different American minorities in most regions of the country. Surely, the absence of true literacy and creative vocal expression among minorities, working-class whites, and a significant percentage of the rest of the students combine to make it an inexcusable waste of human resource.

Subsequently, time-honored tradition set in motion school policies that encourage few students to learn a second language. Conversely, the commonality has been encouraged and nurtured to regard as socially unworthy any member of a foreign group who may speak or retain his native language.[62] Given the antagonistic historical sequences between

69

Spain and England, in concert with the imposition of the Black Legend curse on the brown American Spanish-surnamed whose antecedents were most ironically the victims, the odious and antagonistic sentiments reserved for Spanish speakers is especially more deep-rooted and pronounced.

That Chicanos inherited the enemies of Spain and of Mexico is superfluous. This terrible legacy is manifest in the vile treatment accorded brown Americans as sanctioned or governed by their Hispano Mexican Spanish-speaking, Catholic culture and way of life. For the latter psychologically oppressive and apartheid-like treatment is more particularly widespread and common in the Southwestern United States. Either a brown skin or a Spanish surname stigmatizes an individual with the labels of opprobrium—Mexican—Catholic.

The core of American civilization is secular humanist in foundation and orientation. Its naturalistic and deistic roots evolved in conjunction with a notably anti-Christian and anti-Catholic religio-philosophical twist. It was only natural given the age and the ideological forces at work at the time. However, as Anglo-American civilization extended its frontiers westward it also became religiously anti-Indian. For guided by Eurocentric secular humanistic principles of reason, its naturalistic subjectivism, which is prone to error because it can easily be swayed by emotional content, corrupted the lofty concepts of natural law in a relativistic sway that ran amok. Indians had basic human rights, too based on the laws of nature, but not as skewed by renegading white Americans.

The Indians and their blood brothers, the Mexicans, were barriers to white American civilization. Some could be regenerated and taught the way of the white race, but to regenerate them all was never the plan because it was not feasible. Anyway, American civilization was the modern cradle of man's return to the notion and the law of the survival of the fittest. Competition was the new way. The major hurdle for the so-called Indian and the Mexican was their political powerlessness. Whites had control of all the agencies of power and of freedom, including that of law enforcement which protected that power and that freedom. Moreover, the white man had no intention of sharing his institutions of freedom with the Indians or the Mexicans.

---

62. This attitude prevails among educators despite the fact countless studies conclusively show the majority of American students would welcome the opportunity to learn a second language.

American citizens are guaranteed religious freedom by a written constitution. The public schools by law, therefore, cannot espouse or teach a given theological doctrine. Nevertheless, critics charge that while no denominational religion is cultivated, a notable anti-dogmatic blend, a heterodoxy of an amorphous Christianity and secular humanism, is advocated and promoted. The former's reference is to the peculiar syncretism described by some scholars as a status quo civil religion, republican protestantism or Christo-republicanism.[63]

The negative impact of this religio-philosophical doctrine on traditional religion and cultures is devastating. The sectarian theological-philosophical composite that comprises the materialistic and racially exclusive monocultural foundations of "false" Americanism's "melting pot" ideology undercuts dogmatic supernatural religion. Hence, given this narrow exclusive secular design, is it any wonder the schools systematically cultivate religiously indifferent students? It could hardly be otherwise in a secular state that separates church and state, and in which the state is in an endless philosophical war with dogmatic religion.

However, a declaration of this nature cannot fully be appreciated unless we accept the reality that religious indifference is honed by monocultural secular humanistic and subjective relativistic training and inducement. Sequentially, this process promotes godlessness and paves the road to agnosticism, and inextricably to atheism. Frankly, the negative psychological impact and alienation secularism spawns among brown American and Mexican Catholic children is no less devastating than it is among white American Catholics. But there is one vital difference. Because brown young people do not yet possess the same range of freedom as whites, they have not become nor are they yet potentially as dissident and as hedonistic as Anglo-Americans of any race or gender.

A distinguished and critical American educator succinctly wrote that the schools are guilty of a "brutal intolerance of deep feeling between persons of emotional commitment to others," and, that ". . . love (and) loyalty, are violations of its code and are severely punished." In their quest to individualize personalities, the schools de-personalize

---

63. See B. C. Orozco, *Republican Protestantism in Aztlan, passim,* pp. 53–71.

and "break up what it calls . . . cliques which it sees as anti-democratic and potential perilous sources of resistance and subversion."[64]

The Chicano corporeate personality is currently caught in the throes of this uncompromising process; a process in which his sociopsychological construct is being assailed, tested, and severely shaken. White American status quo expectations demand that communal oriented brown Americans yield to an individualized, self-centered social pattern. That means that Chicanos and Mexican Americans must alter their way of thinking, speaking, believing, and behaving in order to fit the expected reconstruct.

Educational specialists are fully aware that a secularized ego ideal that fails to compensate for diminished ego strength, lost by enforced deculturation or aversive conditioning methods, for example, potentially can spawn emotionally demoralized and deviant personalities. However, despite this clear and significant indicator the school's sociopsychologically crippling monocultural anti-Hispano Mexican alienation agenda marches on.

With all of this in mind, and by whatever standard of evaluation or measurement any critic may choose, exculpating the schools' deficient educational design can be monumental and difficult. For little room for debate exists that the social curriculum of the American public school system is horrendously narrow and exclusive. The real tragedy lies in the fact that in the schools' uncompromising quest to mold monocultural conformity and the subordination of the nation's colored minorities, racism, resistant and antagonistic pluralism is the result.

The schools, literally speaking, have created their own monster, for, frankly, the more individualized brown Americans are the persons demanding the alternative programs for Chicanos and asking the self-centered questions: What about me? We are Americans! We are Chicanos! Policy-making groups, evidently, have yet to recognize they are dealing with full-fledged thinking brown Americans. Moreover, they have not been sufficiently alarmed to realize that the country's monoculturalizing, self-centering institutions of learning are persistent initiators and conveyors of human insensitivity, racial disharmony, religious bigotry, and cultural isolation and social antagonisms.

---

64. Edgar Z. Friedenberg, "Status and Role in Education" in Skolnick-Curie's, *Crisis in American Institutions* (Boston: Little Brown and Company, 1973), p. 309.

Finally, judiciously evaluating the Chicano experience in the afore-mentioned educational philosophical context affords considerable credence to activist Chicano allegations that the schools purposefully drive brown students out, or fail them. Surely if the schools don't build on what children bring to school, then the institutions must obviously be driving them out. Indeed, those Chicano scholars devoid of iniquity concur that the schools have been fundamentally responsible for the astronomical dropout rate and turning the country's Mexican Americans away from education.[65]

THE NEED FOR HOST SYMBOLISMS IN THE SCHOOLS

Most education specialists agree with the sound educational adage that if the purpose of the schools is to develop the child's cultural and mental skills, then a curriculum should be structured to meet the child's potential as it relates to the psychological condition of the particular child. Since, in fact, an educated citizenry is essential and critical to the economy and body-politic of the United States, a new and complete guidance plan, reason would dictate, should be mandated.

By the very nature of the Chicano experience careful selection of teachers is indicated. Prerequisites for teachers who teach large numbers of brown barrio or Mexican children should include racial sensitivity and a profound ethnic awareness of the group. To seek understanding without intensive training or a comparable social experience is educationally unrealistic. Employment of persons of similar ethnic background and race is not always possible, nor necessary. The alternative in such cases, therefore, is intensive training for non-ethnics who propose or expect to teach so-called Hispano-Mexican ethnics.

In this regard, positive attitudinal changes have been observed in schools where brown Americans are represented on secretarial and teaching staffs as counselors and as custodians. Also, communication between the Chicano community and school personnel markedly improves. Where these social components are lacking, communication

---

65. Professor Julian Nava was the first Mexican American to be elected to the Los Angeles City Schools' Board of Education. Nava served from 1966–1978. In 1978, following twelve years of firsthand observation, Nava, a conservative and not openly pro-Chicano Movement Harvard University Ph.D., analyzed that the "schools alienate Chicano students." That they "teach them how to be disrespectful, to feel worthless; and, that the schools push them out," interview by Ray Gonzales, *Pacesetters,* KTLA, 1978.

is poor, and the dropout rate among Chicanos is high, attendance is irregular, little ambition for future training is observed, and parent interest is poor and indifferent.

The ideal solution lies in empathetic and sensitive teachers and teaching. Jaime Escalante, a foreign transplant, who pursued teaching as a second career, proved that barrio youngsters can learn to perform academically, in spite of their negative social school experience and the inculcated culture of denial, even as late as in high school. The feature film portraying Escalante's incredible success, "Stand and Deliver," is well-depicted and self-explanatory.

Despite the media's lame and dishonest objective in striving to make this marvelous personality appear to be a "super teacher," because he was able to teach "Mexican" kids advanced academic material, Escalante has always maintained that his brown calculus students all possessed the intelligence and capacity to learn and to succeed. And, that he simply stimulated and cultivated that potential and capacity. Well, all that may very well be true, but it certainly can make a difference when a teacher breaks the culture of denial and ignorance teaching cycle by raising the self-worth of brown students; and, by informing them that their indigenous ancestors invented the concept of zero in mathematics.[66]

THE GENERATION AND CULTURAL GAPS

The senior high school generally offers a less demanding and more flexible social environment than found in the middle school. Nonetheless, the social value systems, the white status symbols, the conflict and anxiety cues of psychological humiliation learned via deculturation and open ethnic vilification remain unchanged. In high school cultural and racial antagonisms become more subtle than previously in the student's experience. Hence, as would be expected, heightened adolescent anxiety and aggression brings the conflict to a head in various ways that we shall explore.

---

66. Mr. Escalante left the Los Angeles City Schools in 1991 prompted by a lack of support from the district's teacher's union and from administrators. He made it clear, nonetheless, that a lack of positive self-images and self-worth among brown students are major causes for their lack of motivation to learn, and for the high dropout rate. Interview with Mr. Escalante, June, 1989. See also the *Los Angeles Times,* March 3, 1990.

By tenth grade most brown youngsters have learned a place of delegated social inferiority. Most realize they are seen and treated differently because their presence is unappreciated. Eventually most come to grips with the multiple reasons for which they are socially subordinated and excluded. Chicanos gradually discover that the school setting is but a microcosm of real life beyond the limited confines of a school campus which expects a subordinated minority response. So, by this stage in their education barrio young people know they are socially fixed outcasts and second-class citizens in the white cultural scenario.

So, arguably, by the end of senior high school the differential socialization of most majority group students is well-seated in their minds. Inclusive in that process is the previously discussed hardening of anti-Mexican and anti-Spanish attitudes which are a viable part of the American heritage learned in school. Notwithstanding these foolish obstacles, Chicano youngsters are further burdened by the natural growth and development problems of adolescence. Adolescents experience difficult periods of adjustment as they journey from childhood to adulthood. Chronological growth and maturation varies in intensity among adolescents. But, generally, it is gradual and normal for most adolescents as they sever the primary group bond, and are well on the road to maturity by their late teens.

A Chicano youngster is still expected to forsake his subordinated countercultural primary group characteristics, even his accommodating bicultural background, as a prerequisite for entering the Anglo majority world. Thus, he is expected to enter the theoretically pluralistic Anglo-American one-dimensional culture as a brown, Spanish surnamed non-Chicano. The added burden and psychological pressures of cultural alienation during adolescence, which itself is an intensive marginal period during which much individualized internal conflict is present, severely compounds a brown student's emotional problems. Because of the harsh and insensitive approach to his ethnicity it makes a mentally healthy adaptation to the hostile Anglo school environment doubly difficult.

Although each personality is distinctive, a general consensus among educators supported by countless studies suggests adolescence is a period of rapid maturation during which young minds are susceptible to a multiplicity of forms of unstable expression; often contradictory behavior at its finest. For example, while most adolescents strongly desire adult approbations, they not uncommonly provoke the very treatment they most abhor by their puerile behavior. Barrio Chicano adolescents are not particularly different in this regard except perhaps in extant manifestation.

More troublesome is the fact brown American adolescents, given all their maturation problems, coincidentally experience considerable ethnic vilification and aversive training. They find themselves caught in the unrelenting whirlwind process of uncompromising deculturation and marginalization. Brown American scholars inform us that as these young people seek the acceptance of white peers and teachers as American, many are subtly rejected because they look like Mexicans and do not fit the stereotypical American image, obviously because they are not white. Therefore, brown youngsters are compelled to endure a triple burden of, first, simply growing up; second, desocialization and the deprivation of their culture; and third, the rapid, but peripheral socialization into the other.

Processing young colored skinned people through the so-called "melting pot" experience is beset by numerous negative ramifications. European immigrant children had severe problems of social adjustment at the turn of the century, but entrance and blending into American life was facilitated by racial affinity. Not so for the colored races of Africa, the Western Hemisphere, and Asians. They remain most un-American regardless what generation American-born they may be. The following chapter delves into *bato loquismo* as a dark side of the American ethnocide process, and what drives otherwise normal children to such violent anti-social behavior as they mature as counter-subcultural misfits in Chicano and American society.

CHAPTER 9

Later Adolescence and the Dark Side of Ethnocide:

The *Bato Loco* Fantasy

The general barrio practice of granting young men measurable freedom and responsibility by early adolescence invariably presents a common cue for "cultural conflict." Many brown American barrio adolescents find it puerile to be treated like children in school, while they are treated more like adults in barrio society. In effect, the contrast in social expectations and treatment accorded them is a point of conflict most unfortunately compounded by the oppressive culture of overtly. This dual community maturation experience can generate Chicano adolescent disdain for white students whom they may regard as childish and wimpish. In view of the separate counter-cultural societies in which they are nurtured, this earned response is only natural.

The longer period of training and consequent period of deferment of gratification demanded by a highly urbanized and industrialized society, militates against early social maturation. It is not at all surprising, therefore, to find that white adolescent behavior often threads on through the middle twenties and in some cases into the late twenties; whereas barrio Chicanos reach social maturity chronologically earlier. Premature termination of school and the lesser period of training demanded for unskilled and semi-skilled labor are other factors that accelerate maturation among brown young people.

A brief examination of the facts reveals that each succeeding brown American generation (there have been only two) has become notably less conventionally "Mexican" or Chicano.[67] Two generations of American urbanization, systematic schooling, the influence of television and competitive social interaction with the dominant group has nurtured a more cosmopolitan, but also, a more dissident, fragmented, politically aware and troubled brown American community.

In the transitional process experiences of many members of the group, a disproportionate number of brown Chicano youth have become markedly more culturally alienated, self-centered, emasculated, and marginalized. Also it has become more socially fractured and distant from its primary host elements. The symbolic world via the Spanish language, the family, their religious values, and the community infrastructure of many of these young people has been vilified and eroded in the exchange.[68]

Chicano adolescence is no less psychologically eventful than it is for white youngsters. As previously noted, turbulent feelings of idealism, love, compassion, uncertainty, and the supersensitivity that besets adolescents also troubles young brown people. The Chicano adolescent endures the same psychological distress, confusion, and anxiety as white American adolescents. However, important differences like poverty, cultural, linguistic, religious, and racial antagonisms aggravate the normal maturation process of Chicanos to a far greater extent than previously realized.

A most vital point in this scenario is that most educators are sensitive to the salient problems of the generation gap and strive to ease the negative social impact that it might have on white adolescents, through guidance activities and curricular changes. But nothing is done for Chicano young people to ease the psychological problems and anguish gen-

---

67. Although Mexican Americans have been an American political reality since 1848, their barrio isolation for one hundred and sixty years, constant immigrant flow from Mexico and their recent opportunity to mainstream, is what gives the group a foreign and immigrant-like character in the eyes of most white Americans.

68. Ironically, the neo-Chicano Movement accelerated Anglo cultural penetration and alienation, and the psychological marginalism of the group by inadvertently undercutting the authority of culture with their subjectivistic relativism. This state of individuated liberation emboldens the subjective secularized brown American gender-centric female and homosexual personality to brashly expound odious narcissistic anti-Chicano and anti-Mexican cultural exasperation often presumed authoritative by the uninformed and ignorant.

erated by social disintegration and marginalization. While Chicano adolescent anxiety and frustration may be theoretically reduced, like it may be among white or Anglo-like students, little thought or consideration is given to his diverse and distinctive non-Anglo background. Little is done about the cultural conflict and shame of being "Mexican" (i.e., brown) promoted by the schools, and experienced by brown students in the throes of deculturation and differential conditioning.

On the contrary, progression through the aversive conditioning reward and punishment process and experience continues to result in feelings of inferiority and negative learning among these young people. Many become severely psychologically damaged; a condition manifest in a most characteristic posture of resignation. Too few of these youngsters ever generate any hope of improving their socio-economic status because subliminally they know little can be done about it.

In view of this psychologically debilitating process it is vile to suggest that the consequences of this values system's clash and breakdown manifest in attitudinal behavior associated with resignation, withdrawal, diffidence, and defeatism, and resistance to achievement, are innate, or "Catholic" traits of the Mexican American people. When, in all candor, it is destructive behavior spawned by teaching counter-cultural secular humanist and subjective relativist values to Catholic idealism on which Chicano and Mexican culture are rooted. Institutionalized ethnic cleansing school policies that suppress and deny Chicanos their self-identity, masculinity, femininity, ethnic expression via their art, music, and literature, as well as their social equality in an American social setting, denies brown Americans the right to exercise their religious freedom as well as their natural right "to be" Chicanos.[69]

Other peculiar modes of behavior more in concert with American behavior are similarly self-evident. The more aware, self-centered,

---

69. Many teachers who in the past denied Chicanos and other colored Americans artistic expression opportunities, while alleging that art was color-blind are openly accenting their antagonistic sentiments to multicultural artistic expression. The former's posture regarding art, i.e., that it should be free of a "political" or "social" agenda smacks of racism. They dismiss the basic concept of creative art whether it is acting, dancing, or painting as being subjective creativity. Politics and social experiences are similarly subjective. Surely, how less subjective is the art mural genius of the Mexican giants Jose Clemente Orozco and Diego Rivera whose communist leanings bred their anti-Spanish, anti-Catholic, and anti-capitalist themes? What nonsense.

The multicultural agenda of some schools is resulting in Chicano themes "offensive" to white racists, because the latter cannot relate to the jarring subjective Chicano world which, incidentally, is the by-product of an oppressive Eurocentric American white social order.

dissident, and often the more assertive Chicano students, learn to be defensive, hostile, and anti-social. Many become disenchanted and assume the demeanor of what is generally referred to by Chicanos as *batos locos* or *cholos*. Frankly, not much better modes of behavior should be expected from an environment inclusive of insensitive teachers, and a school social setting traditionally grounded in the vilification of and spiteful contempt for "Mexicans" (i.e., brown, Spanish surname citizens).

The average brown American student grounded in egalitarianism and blossoming as a subjective relativist gradually concludes that he is denied the hope of being somebody in American society by the schools. But not just somebody as an American, but his natural right of being somebody as a brown American citizen. Again for the aforementioned redundant general reasons: because he is dark-skinned and looks like a "Mexican." This rudimentary and naturally harsh conclusion is supported by substantial documentation and by southwestern American social custom.[70]

CHILD ABUSE AND *BATO LOQUISMO*

The federal government recently defined child abuse: impairing a child's "emotional health" and "emotionally depriving him of his self-worth," says the government, "is child abuse." Now, does this, in effect, implicate the schools' time honored agenda for promoting a culture of denial, its pattern of social and cultural deprivation, and aversive conditioning among Chicanos? Which, by the way, are known conflict and anxiety producing factors that fuel the growth of the more visible anti-social and aberrant social patterns of many Mexican American youth.

That these practices fall well within the range of institutionalized child abuse as defined by the United States government is superfluous. Moreover, how much acumen does it require to conclude that these un-American extremes were never intended to be part and parcel of a free and democratic American public school system, with the primary responsibility of promoting positive civil behavior, egalitarianism, meritorious advancement, and democratic behavior? Oh John Dewey where are you now that we need you?

---

70. *The U.S. Commission of Civil Rights Report,* 1974.

In the barrios Chicano youths who are referred to as *la plebe* or *batos locos*[71] (hoodlums), are socially stigmatized and distinguishable deviant sub-group members connected with *gente baja* (lower class) behavior. In barrio society their perverted sense of identity is identified as an extreme manifestation of depraved egoism and malignant self-centeredness. Frankly, it mirrors a socio-psychological condition wrought by the schools' subjective relativist agenda and abusive anti-Mexican social curriculum; a psychological state of mind any trained educator can identify as one beset by conflict and anxiety; psychological patterns best identified as the foundation stones of behavior pathology.

Bato loco behavior is well known in the barrios, a mode of life governed by violent fantasies and measured by its members' absence of a true sense of community; negative behavior marked and attested to by their relentless and remorseless brown on brown violence. In the barrio community they are the ultimate *brutos,*[72] because they are unrestrained restless social predators. Given this horrid recognition, what are Chicanos expected to do when the troublesome adolescent maniacs and young hostile gang predators are their own brothers and sisters, their own flesh and blood?[73]

In all sincerity, the origin and motivation of their abusive and destructive social behavior is not as well-known to most parents; but parents realize the schools are somehow responsible for their odd conduct. *Las escuelas los hacen bravos* (the schools make them wild) is an oft enough repeated parental phrase that more than suggests they

---

71. The Spanish B and V sounds are the same and, therefore, interchangeable. Thus, it is either *Vato* or *bate*.

72. *Bruto* is an animal. Animals have no souls, feelings of community, or sense of being.

73. Gangs serve as the facilitators for violent fantasies of murder; thus, hostile gang activity has taken on the trappings of psychotic terrorism as a mechanism to control the ambience. The escalating violence in the barrios has brandished new rules that call for a harsher response. The *cholos* have broken the long-established circle of restraint. Now that brown-on-brown violence has led to the senseless killing of innocent children and bystanders, brothers and sisters, parents and relatives have accrued the added responsibility of having to take a more serious rational public stand against their own flesh and blood. This is the most immediate way to stem the violence. Clearly parents must accept the reality that their children are no longer their own.

"This is the only country where we teach children to kill children," observed Edward James Olmos during the Desi Awards in August, 1992. Eighteen years went into the making his movie *American Me*, noted Olmos, "to bring this tragedy to the American public." Mr. Olmos presumes the American public will support whatever action it takes to stop this violent behavior because it cares.

possess that awareness. Nonetheless, because they place unchallenged trust in the schools they fail to pursue their natural instincts to confirm their suspicions, that the schools do revamp their children's basic home training and personal psychology.

In the 1940s the *Pachucos* emerged as the public schools' most infamous "Mexican" anti-social by-products. *Pachucos* were highly demoralized individuated young people who found themselves caught between two antagonistic cultures and values systems. Caught, in effect, in a labyrinth of solitude, emotional despair, and confusion.[74] Remarkably, these odious and somber barrio subcultural elements continue to be spawned by the schools, obviously because the subjective relativist agenda and the anti-Mexican advocacy social curriculum in the schools remains unchanged.

Although the schools' brown deviant by-products are no longer ascribed the *Pachuco* label, their deportment is currently more dangerous and diabolical. Nonetheless, the young thugs' behavior is analogous in many ways with the anti-social culture of denial then evident among the defiant and socially deviant *Pachucos*. Curiously, the current *bato loco* mode of dress parallels that distinctive ideal too. In the early period the latter were identifiable by bell-bottom khaki or blue "county jail" trousers slightly draped, perhaps baggy, with loose cotton T-shirts or plaid shirts.[75]

Presently, among the biosocially arrested personalities, crude and monosyllabic English, pidgin English or Spanish, and an abrasive and hostile demeanor characteristically persists. So does the "mad-dogging" posture technique of intimidation. The dress mode changed by the

---

74. Social scientists continue to dismiss the public schools as the major breeding ground for hostile gangs. Every indicator points to the public schools as the major cause for this perverted and aberrant behavior. The schools are the only institution that competes equally with the home in character formation. It is, in fact, the only institution that has such pervasive psychological control, besides natural parents, over most American children. The proliferation of drugs and gangs, persistent poverty, and continuing racism all contribute to a child's malevolent transformation. Poor family supervision and peer groups are important too, but not as prominently as the schools.

Moreover in the schools, as we noted in examining the elementary level, an absence of father models creates ideal feminization or emasculation conditions, due to the great majority of teachers being female. See Sexton, *The Feminized Male, Ibid,* pp. 96–97.

Professor James D. Vigil misses this point, too, in his otherwise prescient study on gangs. See Vigil, *Barrio Gangs* (Austin: University of Texas Press, 1988).

75. *Bato Loco* graffiti serves as their "declaration of presence and communication" rooted in a psychologically primitive impulse to mark boundaries and to compete.

1980s in most urban centers, and by the 1990s the traditional garb among many was discarded. Consequently, it has become more difficult to identify hostile youth whose dress and hairstyles have become more trendy and spiffy.[76] Black caps, shaved heads, and black jackets have also become more popular.

The so-called *cholas,* cha-cha girls, or *locas* are the female counterparts to the *batos.* They are as demoralized and as socio-psychologically alienated as their male counterparts. Many continue to wear cosmetics with the traditional semi-raccoon exotic mask look, and the "drug-store spiked blond or redheaded look." The object of their distinctively defiant dress modes and demeanor is to brashly set themselves apart from the other students. These rough and tough self-images are socially negative as they are intended to offend. Actually, the violent activities among *batos locos* and the *cholas* are sufficiently self-evident in the streets of many of our urban centers to require further elaboration here.[77]

Given the schools' psychologically abusive social curriculum that de-motivates so many Chicanos, other marginalized and negative patterns of behavior are fueled. However, it is critical to stress that not all brown American students manifest their crippling frustration and anger by withdrawing or becoming openly hostile. The majority of those remaining in school are somehow motivated to accommodate the school's undemocratic social and psychological demands. Also, that a substantial number of these students abjure their race and real self-image is not especially surprising, since most come from conservative, generally stable brown American homes.

---

76. Something of their general character that is not commonly known is the fact they usually hold regular eight-hour jobs during the day. A mode of behavior that strongly suggests they are significantly rational to be able to learn to restrain their violent and murderous impulses and actions.

A point of fact that brings to mind the antecedent warlike tribes of many of these young people who were Christianized by the Catholic missionaries from the sixteenth century onward. Great warriors became men of peace via Christian carnalismo; creating a spiritual unity that led to eventual nationhood. Evidently, in our times stripped of their fraternal values by the schools, discrimination and poverty, many in wrenching despair have assumed a violent cultural lifestyle preference, which subsumes the ritualistic-like killing of other brown persons. Unlike their antecedent tribal warriors who killed to survive, their conscienceless life destroying ritual is more truly a form of suicide.

77. According to Los Angeles county and city police tabulation, gun related deaths mushroomed in Los Angeles county, California, from 210 to 700 in just the decade from 1981–1991. Many of the victims have been brown Americans, usually Chicanos and Mexican immigrants' children.

Few have dared to boast that changing races is a simple or easy matter. To meet white society's social mandates to be white or to look white, many brown American women attempt to cosmetically impress what nature has failed to do. They dye their hair blond or red, and some even attempt to alter their skin color or experiment with other excesses. This comportment reflects simplistic futile efforts that indicts society's imposition on Chicanos of a culture of brown race denial. It is connected with society's pro-white social prerequisites—theoretically to be accepted as Americans.

Furthermore, at this critical stage during the dark side of their personality and character formation, many brown American young people are driven by inordinate self-interest as they become most notably self-centered and openly anti-Mexican. Clearly, some are plagued with such a profound irrational dislike of themselves, that any known affinity with their Mexican racial origins is repressed and in many cases guided to extinction. Unrelenting social pressures in concert with a deep and real fear of relegation to inferiority, drives many to great lengths resulting in a cycle of negative impulsive behavior. In their misguided stress forming quest, they inadvertently burrow more distressful social conditions for themselves.

ATHLETICS AND THE BROWN STUDENT

It is difficult to assess to what degree brown American students might be aware regarding their disadvantage when competing with whites under any social condition. Some of the brighter and more aware young people surely must suppress strong impulses when they are patronized and relegated to social inferiority. Perhaps, it is because so-called "class" in Chicano society is measured by social etiquette standards of behavior and not by material wealth or pretensions of racial superiority, that their rejection by white peers can more easily be tolerated. But despite what would seem adequate psychological armoring, given the social pressures encountered by these youngsters, many of them still develop enormous inferiority complexes.

In this unfriendly social setting they learn that in order to gain a semblance of respect, they must vastly outperform whites on the latter's own ground. Athletic competition offers a unique personal opportunity for some to excel. Chicano athletes know they are not inferior. Physical competition is the name of the game with them. Yet, even in

The barrio language of confusion and self-hate.

Who has encouraged you most to your attending college?

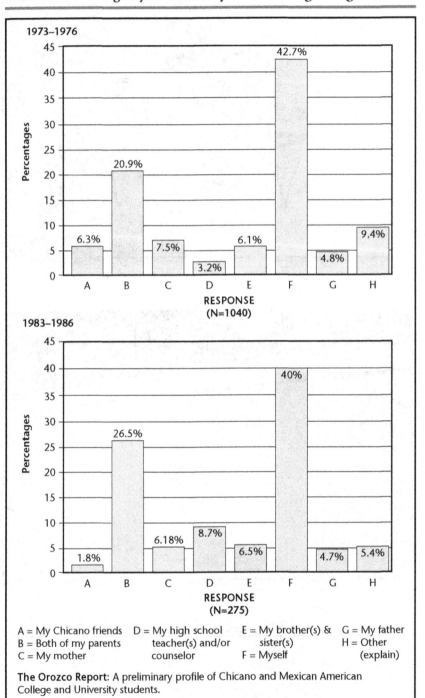

A = My Chicano friends   D = My high school   E = My brother(s) &   G = My father
B = Both of my parents   teacher(s) and/or   sister(s)   H = Other
C = My mother   counselor   F = Myself   (explain)

The Orozco Report: A preliminary profile of Chicano and Mexican American College and University students.

Who has been the greatest source of discouragement to your attending college?

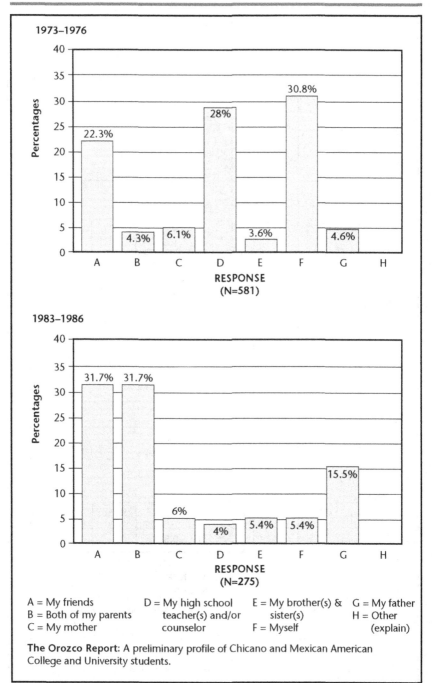

A = My friends
B = Both of my parents
C = My mother

D = My high school
   teacher(s) and/or
   counselor

E = My brother(s) &
   sister(s)
F = Myself

G = My father
H = Other
   (explain)

The Orozco Report: A preliminary profile of Chicano and Mexican American College and University students.

Do you speak and understand Spanish?

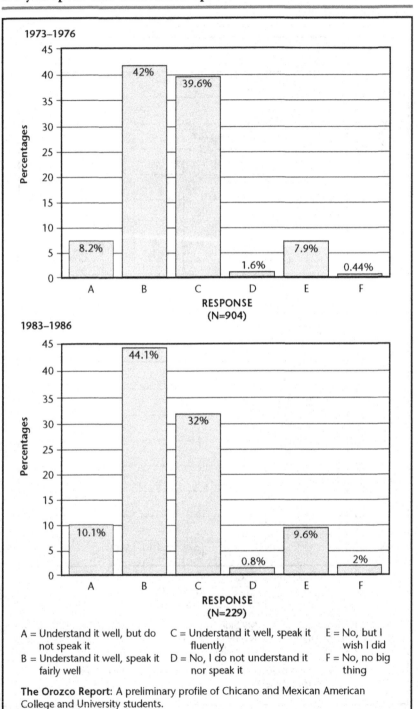

A = Understand it well, but do   C = Understand it well, speak it   E = No, but I
    not speak it   fluently   wish I did
B = Understand it well, speak it   D = No, I do not understand it   F = No, no big
    fairly well   nor speak it   thing

The Orozco Report: A preliminary profile of Chicano and Mexican American College and University students.

competitive athletics brown students encounter discrimination, and often, coarse and degrading humiliation.

Chicanos have been known to drop out of school in noticeable numbers as a result of not making the football and baseball squads. Barrio students are like other young people when it comes to merit. They resent favoritism and unfair practices, because they view them as barriers to opportunity and achievement. Taught to be egalitarian in school they are often surprised to observe teachers not uncommonly violate those very tenets. Another form of rejection, they must assume, intended to discourage them. Prematurely severing school ties is a brown student athlete's prudent face-saving alternative to the unremitting attack of his dignity and psychological self-control.

Coaching young people is serious business given the traditional assumption by many that it helps build character. While many successful coaches are inclined to be egalitarian in reference to racial or ethnic background, many coaches do openly discriminate by playing favorites and discouraging Chicano athletes from competing in any sport. Remarkably, despite the many obstacles, a few southwestern brown American high schoolers, through sheer determination alone, emerge as outstanding all-around athletes, and are a credit to the schools and community they represent.[78]

Frankly, for most, their laudable efforts end ingloriously with graduation. Dreams of being recruited by major universities and colleges are dashed early. In the spectrum of athletic achievement and competition, it is a fundamental fact that the general exclusion of brown American athletes on university and college programs is callous bigotry. Their exclusion lies in sharp contrast to the recruitment of black and white athlete ratios, "Mexicans" are simply not desirable candidates as university athletic heroes. Unlike Mexican Americans, Afro-Americans carry "American surnames" and thereby pass for whites on team rosters, in news releases, and reports. To possess a Spanish surname is a primary cause for the proportionately fewer brown athletes found or seen on university and college rosters.[79]

---

78. In many given parts of the Southwest coaches are forced to play brown American athletes because that is all that is available to them. In other words they have no clear alternative.

79. Just to cite a recent case is the story of John Aguilar of Canyon Country, California. "Memories are all Aguilar has to show for his senior year," wrote a *Los Angeles Times* sports writer. "I just feel puzzled," said Aguilar, "You look at receiving M.V.P of your team, co-M.V.P. of your league, and you are player of the year in the *Los Angeles Times*, and you are thinking: how can I receive all this and not even have a shot of going somewhere?" See *Los Angeles Times*, June 19, 1992. Aguilar ventured east to the Atlantic seaboard where as a walk-on helped turn a losing program around in one season.

In high school, nevertheless, more psychologically detrimental to the proportionately few Chicano athletes, is the humiliating harsh treatment many experience after they somehow manage to make a school team sport. Brown athletes are the brunt of many coaches' jokes, often uttered in a not uncommon quaint twang: "Hurry up, wetback!" "Come on you chili peppers!" "Come on Pancho, is that the way you pick beans?" "That's the trouble with you taco eaters!"

In review, they are racist references intended to humiliate and to lower the self-esteem and status of brown athletes. More injurious to all concerned is that it reinforces stereotypes among whites that brown students are less than American and thereby unequal or inferior. Surely, a better response cannot be expected from white student athletes who tend to follow their coaches' example.[80]

Situations in which brown athletes are subjected to outlandish forms of criticism or ostracism are more common than realized. The highly-motivated superb high school athlete knows his or her capabilities. He or she knows, and everybody else knows, if he or she is superior to whites on the field or on the basketball court. Moreover, competitive successes develop an abundance of self-confidence and self-esteem in these young people, a self-worth that words and intrusive actions cannot easily shake. Talented athletes thrive on success and recognition. Understandably, inasmuch as everyone likes a winner, it is not surprising to learn that successful brown athletes are more readily accepted by whites because of their extraordinary skills.

Ironically, during the height of the Chicano Movement, militant neo-Chicanos rejected and shunned Mexican American athletes as potential active members because many believed brown athletes were too insensitive and accommodating to the White Establishment. In retrospect, they were probably correct given the athlete's accomplished success and acceptance by whites and others. Nevertheless, athletes often possess well-developed leadership characteristics which, with proper guidance, can be effectively utilized as leaders or as models; perhaps as a force for cultivating operant conditioning among Chicano students.

---

80. Little acumen is required to recognize that name-calling left unchecked can contribute to the formation of racist attitudes by whites and to a corresponding anger, and finally to the erosion of self-worth among Chicanos.

With regard to the above observation, a poignant experience can be related to underscore that point. During the East Los Angeles high schools "blow-outs" in 1968, a brown American star basketball player led the protest march in one of the target high schools. For his seemingly un-American actions his coach blackballed him. After playing two seasons for a small sectarian college, he transferred to California State University at Bakersfield where he starred as a guard during the university's two phenomenally successful seasons. This remarkable personality and athlete earned his Master's degree and is presently a successful high school coach and teacher.[81]

A semblance of social status may be the reward for the acquiescing brown pupil or athlete who suppresses his better judgment, and consents to a subordinate status identification as a member of a minority. Inclusive in the accepted delegated role is the expectation that he not complain when a teacher or coach calls him "Pancho" and, that he should laugh at himself when a white teacher or peer calls him a wetback, or a synonymous demeaning label.[82]

In accordance with this unreasonable rationale, it is expected that he do everything required to strengthen his white friends' ego and status, while coincidentally subordinating his own. Thus, through deferential conditioning and psychological disintegration, a Chicano learns to look up to whites because the white's way of life is superior to the "Mexican's," and because the white is the real American, his natural model and his social superior. However, the libertarian questions emerge: Why can't I just be myself in order to be somebody? Why do you have to make an issue about my race and ethnicity?

---

81. Cited from Coach Enrique C. Orozco's recruitment files.

82. A youngster's ability to concentrate is disrupted if he feels alienated and acquires a sense of unworthiness in school. Poor attendance and premature termination are directly related to these sentiments.

CHAPTER 10

A Deplorable
School Record:

Barriers to Being Somebody

onsidered from a psychological standpoint, the senior high
school years are critically fundamental in behavior shaping
and in the making of the Chicano mind. However, differential
socialization and aversive conditioning is an on-going experience. The
process of cultural and emotional disintegration and deprivation, initiated in the elementary school, is continued and reinforced in the middle school years. Thus, operant conditioning for Anglo-Caucasian
dominance in the social life of the high school community remains piv-
otal and is pervasive. Institutionalized social conditions in concert with
other factors combine to heighten the negative psychological tension of
a Chicano's high school experience. Ergo, the astronomical dropout
rate among Chicanos.

Moreover, it is superfluous to suggest that the educational labyrinth
presented here is compounded by insensitivity and uncaring administrators and teachers.[83] A time-honored established curriculum, money-
tight boards of education, deficient teacher training, oversize classes,
paperwork overloads, and unchanging social custom make the problem progressively more formidable and challenging. Nonetheless, extensive corrective groundwork is called for on the primary school level to

---

83. The Los Angeles School District, for example, "does little to hold teachers accountable for
quality of their lessons, and teachers rarely, if ever, are fired for being ineffective educators . . ."
See *Los Angeles Daily News,* March 1, 1992.

more effectively address the problems of minority group adolescence and the bicultural Chicano experience. The problem is not going to go away by itself. Even with some effort, rehabilitating programs or plans never materialize as logically or as effectively as they should, particularly when the effects rather than the causes are treated.

The schools' administrative solution to Chicano education problems lies elsewhere. Traditional approaches or programs in which senior high schools are forced to endure the shortcomings of the intermediate high schools, and required to wrestle with the deficiencies of the elementary schools' program, should be reexamined, reevaluated, and articulated where necessary. Frankly, the education debacle is of such a state of affairs that colleges and universities in more recent times have found themselves burdened by social and educational problems created by public school administrative polices. Socially immature and insensitive professors, the spoon-feeding teaching of many instructors in concert with the pseudo-learning that commonly takes place on college campuses, can hardly be expected to spark ideas or solutions to alleviate deep-rooted student deficiencies of dehumanization and bigotry—the basic problems and attitudes that are cultivated by an ethnocentric and socially supremacist public educational system.

In the past two decades barrio Chicanos are entering colleges and universities in greater numbers for the first time in history. Yet, proportionately the percentages remain very low. Nevertheless, unlike most students they are confronted with social adjustment problems. It is revealing to many concerned individuals to learn that public school and societal attempts to deculturate and to psychologically individualize and to culturally separate these particular students from their host group have, in the main, been partly successful.[84]

White students are not separated from their culture. In fact, white students do well in American institutions because they firmly believe those institutions belong to them. Conversely, Chicanos are not even permitted to carve out their own place within those same institutions.

---

84. *The Orozco Report* showed that between 1973–1976 nearly thirty percent of all brown college and university students were non-barrio reared. By the 1983–1986 survey the percentage had grown to forty-nine percent. Based on this progression, it is safe to speculate that by 1993 the non-barrio brown American ratio should leap to well over sixty percent. These figures reflect two changes. First, more Mexican Americans live outside the barrios due to a diminished racism, and the affordable housing that is available to them.

Among many, a lack of normal social adjustment and a superficial socialization to Anglo life is self-evident. Comparatively, a notable deficiency of academic and linguistic training and preparation for college is also highly evident among students of all races.

Yet, despite some deficiencies many Chicanos have actually earned college and university degrees. The road to success, however, has required intensive guidance and tutorial assistance but fails to see the connection between the achievement and success of the very few as proof that the secondary schools have failed to truly educate the many.

Most educators unrealistically cling to the defunct theory that "Mexican" student failure is rooted in an inborn natural "Mexican" incapacity or in their culture. After all, comes the response, "we are trying to make Americans of them, not Mexicans." Whatever hypothesis they may prefer, statistically Chicanos know that an incredible waste of human talent and energy in the world's most free and progressive society is nothing less than a severe indictment of the American public school system as a system that knowingly fails its colored students.

THE QUESTION OF RELEVANCY

The Orozco Report sheds some light on what brown college and university students consider the actual causes for high school success or failure.[85] In the 1973–1976 survey to the question: "Who has been the greatest source of discouragement to your attending college?" thirty percent of the respondents blamed themselves. Twenty-eight percent of the same group blamed their high school teachers and counselors! Finally, twenty-two percent blamed their friends. (See illustrations on page 87 for comparison with 1983–1986.)

Conversely, to the question, "Who encouraged you the most to your attending college?" forty-two percent assumed personal credit for that decision. Thirty-one percent claimed their parents encouraged them, but, only 9.4 percent credited their teachers and counselors. (See illustration on page 86 for comparison with 1983–1986 survey.)

---

85. *The Orozco Report* is a college and university Chicano and Mexican American attitudinal survey. It covered two periods, 1973–1976 and 1983–1986. The institutions surveyed included the following: California State University, Los Angeles, California State, Northridge, Los Angeles Valley College, Pasadena City College, East Los Angeles College, and Los Angeles City College. It covered the four corners of the City of Los Angeles.

Were you raised in a Barrio?

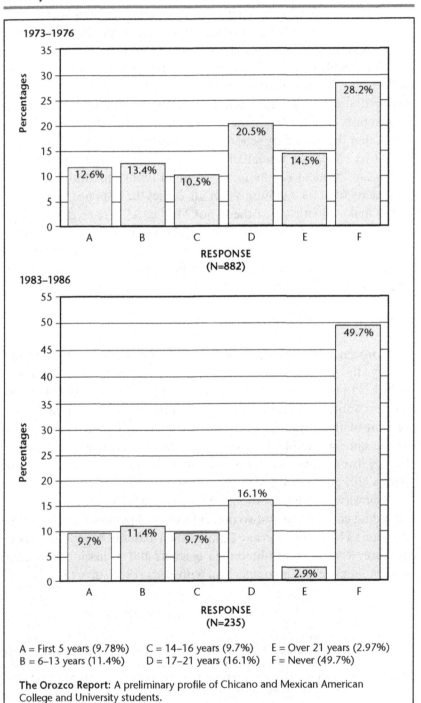

A = First 5 years (9.78%)   C = 14–16 years (9.7%)   E = Over 21 years (2.97%)
B = 6–13 years (11.4%)   D = 17–21 years (16.1%)   F = Never (49.7%)

The Orozco Report: A preliminary profile of Chicano and Mexican American College and University students.

Eighty percent of the respondents profiled in the report were American-born citizens. Eighty-one percent were reared in a barrio for a part or all of their formative years. Over ninety percent claimed to understand Spanish, while the majority knew it well enough to speak it. A most revealing point is the realization that a bicultural bilingual background did not appreciably hinder or retard the academic ambitions of the surveyed group. The number of respondents who were graduates of private and parochial schools was not ascertained. (See illustration on page 88 for percentages of knowledge of Spanish.)

Much ado is made in today's schools regarding social class and educational development. Much is also said regarding value orientations, lack of supportive behavior from family and peer groups, and also of the lack of native ability of the Chicano. Lamentably, even the most sympathetic white educators and writers invariably place the blame for failure on the Chicano student, his family, or his cultural background. Fortunately, there is a more focused side of the issue.

A young female student wrote the following about her school experience:

> When I went to high school, I noticed that many of the Chicanos were gang members. I didn't see the school do anything but punish them for what they were. These are the schools' problems I feel they are partially responsible. They are so busy punishing and kicking these kids out of school that they don't realize they are the cause of it all. Students are likely to be followers and when they don't have anybody to look up to, like a teacher, they tend to follow other students. Even the bad students. The schools tend to discourage these kids from going to college or bettering themselves. Instead they just try to get them to graduate and then go off and do whatever they want. I remember a counselor talking to me about marriage. "Yvonne, you'll just get married, so you probably won't end up going to college. It's very common in your culture, you know? I felt that because I was Mexican American, I had no place in college. Thank God, I never listened to what people say I can't do, but many of those kids in gangs do. They're filled with negativity by the schools that they probably think it's a waste of time to try to be successful. To help, the schools should better encourage these kids. Build up their self esteem and morale. Maybe set up student groups so they can work to better themselves.

Instead of kicking them out, how about asking them, "What's the problem?" Then try to help solve it![86]

For obvious reasons little is made of the schools' on-going anti-Mexican social curriculum and environment, or the negative and counter character formation role played by the children's substitute parents, the teachers. Even less is said of poverty, and as the girl above wrote, the school's failure to develop the self-worth and brown pride of Chicano children. Failure to address these variables when analyzing the formation of damaged personalities and emasculated character, makes any "off-the-cuff" conclusion or assumption ludicrous and worthless.

Besides, in the course of events, graduates who feel they are socially, ethnically, linguistically, religiously, and emotionally deficient and short-changed many years later when they mature, are firmly convinced that is the case. Most high school graduates soon learn they have been inadequately prepared for any suitable vocation or immediate employable profession on entering the competitive work force directly out of high school.

Professionally, it has often been stressed, at least by some educators, that the success of the mass public education curriculum should not be totally determined or guided by the achievement of the small percentage of Chicanos who remain in school. Rather, without being redundant, it has also been emphasized that the large number of dropouts and the negative attitude nurtured toward school by the schools themselves among brown youths, mandates re-analysis and revision of the schools' offerings and social directives.

Corrective and progressive measures call for practical and realistic change; that is, if the cultures and races discussed here are to integrate.

---

86. Cited from author's student files, February, 1992.

The Los Angeles City Schools again take the lead in absurdity. While the city is besieged with gang violence beyond imagination, it finds it more politically expedient to "teach homosexuality in the classroom, and to promote and advocate that form of behavior via senior proms for homosexuals, to young people" many of whom are gender preference vulnerable, rather than to energetically help to resolve the senselessness and endless killing in the streets in their neighborhoods. See the *Los Angeles Times,* June 23, 1992.

Little doubt exists among experts on gang activity that the schools should do a great deal more to alter the violent behavior of these young people. Positive behavior can be taught, just like many have lobbied for laws to teach more tolerant attitudes toward homosexual behavior, although the latter represents such a miniscule proportion of the student body and does not particularly lead to offensive street terrorism and violence.

Indeed, real care could more realistically lead to, and result in, true assimilation. However, that has never been a practical goal of the schools nor of the community at large. Present school policy officially promotes the separation, as opposed to the integration, of American colored and ethnic minorities. Major responsibility, therefore, for change rests with legislators, school boards, and school officials, the managers of state and national political interests, who lamentably are not always sensitive to alternative educational needs.

On the other hand, the degree to which Chicano parents may be aware of the cultural and linguistic barriers confronted by their children is not known. Theoretically, even if they did know, the brown American community does not yet possess the political unity and clout [except in New Mexico] to effectively influence the development of a relevant social curricula and school policy anyway. History has demonstrated that any positive white leadership response to that eventuality is highly problematical.

Surely, the school community and its political response to militant Chicano student school boycotts and anti-school demonstrations, in the recent past, has been negligible while this form of pressure has resulted in the implementation of educational remedies in the larger metropolitan school districts like Los Angeles, San Antonio, and Albuquerque. Meaningful or positive long term change has rarely been forthcoming.

UNNATURAL NATURAL RIGHTS: A WHITE ARISTOCRACY

School boycotts and aggressive community demands in the past two decades has sought the inclusion of plans for more Chicano teachers, administrators, and a relevant academic and social curriculum. Even at this writing Mexican American militants, idealist and activist, are guarded in their hope that brown Americans will in the future be included in the American panorama and process as full-fledged Americans without unreasonable qualification.

The violent overthrow of the American secular humanist capitalist system promoted by segments of the neo-Chicano Movement that turned Marxist Socialist, is a distant and presumably forgotten passion. Nevertheless, it is thought-provoking to ponder when the next community reaction will recur in the event implemented educational remedies fail to sufficiently relieve the social and psychological apartheid pressures. Inclusive of the real pressures such as the relegation of brown Americans to second class citizenship, and the unbroken generation of the debilitating social problems connected with cultural disintegration and alienation.[87]

American social trends support our belief that white American students will continue the social ostracism of Chicanos, and that racism and prejudice toward the group will not disappear in the immediate future. Furthermore, it is reasonably predictable that the poverty-stricken brown population will not find a measure of relief within the margin of this period unless they acquire equitable major political power. Finally, there is little prospect the public schools will alter their policy of rapidly and uncompromisingly stripping Chicanos of every significant vestige of Mexicanism; the psychological and social disorders notwithstanding.

Even the guarded and limited implementation of bilingual programs, intended to help some brown students bridge the cultural gap, is regrettably being met with considerable unprovoked hostility by whites and marginalized ethnics. Little acumen, therefore, is required to surmise that the schools' design for psychological individuation and deculturation, attendant with all its end-products, will continue. This stark reality is the principle cause for dissident and radicalized brown Americanism. It heightens a hostile political sense that has motivated many colored Americans to anticipate a day of reckoning with republican capitalism and white-American supremacism.[88]

Given the fact that the United States is a democratic republic and theoretically not a repressive police state, the parallel with the social unrest and emerging fervent ethnic expression for freedom in many former totalitarian Russian states, after decades of their harsh suppression, is startling. In the countries under control of the Soviets, ethnicity

---

87. A vital question: Was the 1992 "No Justice, No Peace Riot" in Los Angeles a representative tip of the iceberg? Surely the allusion via national television by young black militants, after the rioting, to the United States Declaration of Independence which encourages freedom from oppression is noteworthy.

The number of barrio reared Chicanos who enroll in colleges and universities is diminishing again. Increasingly more of the brown students enrolling in higher education are non-barrio born and reared. These non-barrio brown students see themselves as other than Chicano or Mexican, although whites persistently consider them "Mexican" or Chicano. See *The Orozco Report* illustration on page 96.

88. During the 1992 "No Justice, No Peace Riots" in Los Angeles many colored youths, black and brown, vented their rage in the streets by burning and looting.

was suppressed for the good of the state. Bolshevism stripped all new comrades of their national identity, of any cultural memory, and of their religion and history. Soviet communism alleged to transcend race, gender, language, nationality, and culture. Assimilation to totalitarianism meant all these things. It required that all comrades surrender their individuality "to become nobody" in the new communist social order of nobodies.

Theoretically, Chicanos are deculturated and gradually monoculturalized in a similar fashion for the good of the greater body politic. But in the United States they are individualized with a different goal in mind; presumably to give them a chance "to be somebody" in the American cosmopolitan social order known as the melting pot. However, brown American citizens in actuality are not permitted to be "somebody" because they are of Mexican descent, colored and objectified as a despised foreign ethnic "group." Therefore, its members are perpetually postured as "nobody" in American society regardless of accomplishments.[89]

Psychologically oppressive "false" Americanism, with its melting pot racial and cultural supremacist tenets, remarkably has, nonetheless, spawned the rise and perpetuation of numerous ethnic movements in the country; but none with the future potential gravity of the indigenous Mexican American neo-Chicano Movement. There is little room for debate that American nativism does its separatism handiwork well in our public schools.

---

89. Foreign peoples like many Filipinos are not as discriminated against and invariably are ranked socially higher than native Chicanos by most white Americans, although both groups are generally dark-skinned, Catholic, and possess Spanish surnames.

CHAPTER 11

The Internal Colony Labyrinth:

Perpetuating the Consciousness of Inferiority

Once a barrio Chicano leaves school, either as a graduate or as a dropout, he sets in motion a long subconscious reduction of negative self-images and expectation cues learned and reinforced in school. The adverse psychological effects the public school experience normally has on Chicano children are fourfold.

First, most brown persons never successfully reduce the conflict cues appreciably to overcome personal feelings of racial, cultural, linguistic, social, or religious inferiority nurtured in the schools. Second, most brown Americans never completely eradicate the desire or impulse of white aspiration impressed in school. Third, the fixed emotional state or inclination to wish to please white Americans, or to be accepted by them on their terms, is never totally eradicated or harmonized. And finally, the brown person must somehow find himself as a Chicano or a brown American on his own.

The obstacles to achieving self-identity, self-worth, and psychological consonance are formidable because of the monocultural and monoracial domination complex imposed on him. Brown American personalities are expected to forever feel defensive about being brown-skinned, "Mexican," bilingual, Catholic, and members of a lower socioeconomic class. Logically, the degree of inferiority cue reduction determines for most the margin of psychological maturity and subsequent social equilibrium regained in later life.

In just eleven short years the public schools' counter-cultural agenda shakes the emotional, psychological, and religious character of most youngsters from the underclass and from the barrios. Our public schools literally make demons of many of the Chicano community's brightest youngsters, who blossom by filling the ranks of violent gangs, jails, and prisons. The astronomical dropout rate fuels the endless social problem.

Institutionalized monocultural castigation and rejection for many Chicanos culminates at age seventeen. Seventeen represents the age at which a considerable number prematurely terminate their schooling. They quietly sever the cord with the hostile social environment that has deluded and demoralized them with unrealistic negative self-images and expectations. Reduction of aversive conditioning cues begins at this point and generally plateaus for most by their middle twenties. However, they remain functional *agabachados* in varying degrees forever because they are burdened with the pathological impulses to reactivate the conflict situation in their symbolic behavior. For once an impulse is chronologically nurtured and developed, it can no longer be fully repressed.

This psychological phenomenon explains why so many marginal brown Americans have highly developed weak impulse controls. Many possess nagging negative self-images and grow into what they have been expected to be as adults. Envy, self-hate, low self-esteem, a chip-on-the-shoulder, and an antipathy toward brown Americans and Mexicans are all manifestations of an alienated and coarse instinct level marginal brown American personality—a personality type insidiously cultivated by the schools' deculturation and self-centering process.

These callous instinct level behavioral traits are observable even among neo-Chicanos who have achieved a relatively high degree of ethnic and racial self-awareness and assertive pride. It almost seems as if a substantial part of their native creativity and reason is paralyzed. A point of fact and interest that makes it appear, to those persons who are more aware, that the former are victims of their own stupidity. While in actuality they, like many others, are blinded to the reality. Consequently, they get caught in a kind of pluralistic or collective ignorance.

The Brown Anglo-Saxon Protestant (B.A.S.P.) Aspirant typology discussed in this study is a marginal personality with highly developed functional socio-physiological impulses acquired to survive as an Anglo-American. While this brown American psychological dimension is more precisely the product of non-barrio experiences, barrio Chicanos and Mexicans are not beyond being susceptible to becoming marginal as well. However, whatever its origins, marginalism does fracture the immense political potential and cohesion of any ethnic group. Once a marginal personality becomes culturally alienated and antipathetic to ethnic bonds, reconciliation to primary ethnic psychological patterns from which it was severed during its formative years and youth is difficult.

Countless unimaginable critical factors in the determination of the actual reduction of negative cues exist. They run the gamut of the variability of human character, the profundity of frustration (desocialization), and the depth or degree of aversive conditioning. Moreover, total conscious repression of character responses acquired during the formative years is impossible. Indeed, many of the action-responses impressed and repressed during that chronological stage occur incidentally and unconsciously. In other words, the so-called reflexive actions that are the passive or involuntary forms of behavior are fixed.

A marginal personality may be able to discard or repress only those externals or that overt behavior of which the subject is consciously aware. A great part of the actual self is subconscious, thereby making it more difficult to identify and to extinguish. The subconscious has been adequately described as:

> . . . The abode of everything that is latent, the reservoir of everything that passes unrecorded or unobserved. It contains, for example, such things as all our momentarily inactive memories, and it harbors the springs of all our obscurely motivated passions, impulses, likes, dislikes, and prejudices; our intentions, hypothesis, fancies, superstitions, persuasions, convictions, and in general all of our non-rational operations come from it . . . it is also the fountainhead of much that feeds our religion.[90]

Focused consciousness, therefore, and diffused awareness are sufficiently impotent to convince one another. Much meaningless action can and is produced by them. In the Chicano movement, much paralysis of action was produced by them. The real binding force is the Hispano-Mexican corporate bond or spirit which is the channel for

---

90. Elwin L. House, *The Psychology of Orthodoxy* (New York: Fleming Revel Co., 1913), pp. 62–63.

communication within the multidimensional Mexican American entity. A very fine Mexican Christian ethic binds all Mexicans under a common spirit of La Raza; a subjective core reality most Mexicans recognize as *amor propio*. This corporate reality ethnic dignity escaped most neo-Chicanos because of their self-centeredness, and because their link with the past had been severed. Moreover, the frustrating rage or passion that engulfed many in their quest for a Chicano identity clouded their judgment.

A QUEST FOR CULTURAL CONSONANCE

However, as brown Americans objectify or self-actualize like late-bloomers, a significant number become enlightened. Subsequently, many do attain a realistic assessment of the self-identity problem. They learn that the fundamental barrier to being full-fledged American is neither the parent social environment nor their bilingualism, religion, or imagined negative "Mexican" characteristics. Rather, many reluctantly arrive at a point of having to admit to themselves that the problem is rooted in a twisted and corrupted inner logic impressed in school by monocultural and racist design. A social design anchored by a calculated individuation strategy, in concert with an insidious impression of psychological apartheid attitudes.

Thus, as Chicanos mature emotionally, many realize that having attended public school was a negative experience, and for many, a terrible waste of time. Realistic introspection leads to an awareness that the schools failed to educate them in the fundamentals necessary to advance socially and politically in white American society, as equals and as Chicanos. In effect, they leave school improperly prepared to live a materially successful and productive life in an anti-Mexican white dominated society.

A sense of maturity and self-confidence in ethnic or racial awareness can occur at varying levels of personality development; it also may never occur. If absent in the adolescent years, it may suddenly find expression or synthesis at a time of individual crisis during which the individual is forced to undergo some form of ethnic introspection. A personal intersocial human experience potentially can actuate considerable reflection of an individual's ethnic and racial affinities. It can arise at any time.

Most Mexican Americans experience a crisis of the latter character during adolescence. But due to a dearth of ethnic information available to them, and the schools' active reshaping process, critical personal enlightenment is retarded. The emergence and maturity of a mentally healthy brown self-awareness is hindered. The prohibitive scenario for personal self-awareness described above is out of mode in a society that is the intellectual epitome of the Age of Enlightenment, because it leads to retrogressive behavior and action, like dropping out of school. Be that as it may, leaving school prematurely is personal character survival, for it actuates and accelerates the reduction of negative self-identity and expectation cues learned in school.

The cue reduction process which is analogous to drug addiction withdrawal, while painfully slow, can be a positive reconstructing experience. However, to achieve the ultimate good, brown people must exhaust inordinate amounts of human energy in psychological withdrawal, or in mental blocking. This is due to the profundity of the psychological process their circumstances force them to undergo. Personality construction is an endless human process entailing countless years of growth and maturation. For this reason, intensive study of the historical sequences and evolution of La Raza to comprehend the Chicano, is doubtless psychologically beneficial and liberating.

The transitional brown American personality may ultimately regain or acquire only a superficial understanding of himself, and of the role he has been conditioned and relegated to play, even with a significant and healthy reduction of these cues. Realistically, any normal person's biosocial training and psychology cultivates and sustains a weakened character plateau once it is weakened or corrupted during the formative years.

Brown American personalities weakened or damaged in this manner are doomed to an emotional dependency condition, inclusive of the need to seek the commendation and attention of white Americans. Therefore, as socially disintegrated and weakened characters they are deprived of strong resistance impulses, or of normal fortified inclinations to effect independent thought processes and actions. A sense of personal integration and the potential to think for themselves is never developed or lost. In actuality, they find themselves devoid of their inherent right to self-determination and individual freedom. But, then, in retrospect, this is the major objective of the schools pernicious systematic ethnocide policies and differential conditioning of Mexicans and of their presumed superiors.

In the process they are subject to worse pitfalls. The potent human instincts of pride, envy, lust, gluttony, sloth, anger, and greed are turned loose; and, are enjoined in the individualizing spirit of secular humanism and marginalism. The so-called "melting-pot" process sanctions that inevitability. That these base human instincts overwhelm and grip many vulnerable brown Americans is redundant; lamentably, too often in their most negative manifestations.

Hostile and violent gang activity is the most evident expression of displaced hostility. This belligerent social behavior is devoid of a sense of community, for it denies true self out of fear, shame, or ignorance. These persons are among the most socially displaced and extreme brown marginal personalities, for the basis of their frustration and anger is energized by marginalism and ethnic self-hate. In all truth, it is a horrid condition usually crowned by the cruel humiliation of social exclusion.[91]

Envy promotes political division. Gluttony, sloth, and lust are manifest in drunkenness, drug addiction, exaggerated manliness, and Don Juanism; multi-disordered activity that negatively influences and further disrupts mentally healthy cultural cues and behavior. Frankly, human impulses formerly held in check by Mexican and Chicano cultural norms and values are severely tested and frequently debased. The vast numbers of damaged and disoriented spirits resultant of psychologically disintegrated marginal brown persons is self-evident. Moreover, these problems parallel the disproportionate medical problems in addition to the shorter life span of barrio Mexican American men and women.

THE SOCIAL PROGRAM OF CHICANO SUBORDINATION

A brief historical examination of the traditional negative treatment accorded Mexicans and Chicanos points to a much denied longstanding social plan to keep the brown American and other colored peoples subjugated, or at least psychologically subservient to the dominant white group. This long-standing social posture and practice,

---

91. What primitive or base biochemical changes are stimulated in the brains of brown school-children by the schools that causes the malevolent transformation of many of these youngsters remains to be studied. Whatever the case may be, it is no mystery that a very perverse metamorphosis occurs when a smiling, happy, respectful youngster turns into a disrespectful, hate-filled, demonical gang terrorist bent on killing his own kind. In short, a *bruto* whose conscience, love of family, and sense of community is extinct.

regrettably, is an irrefutable monocultural matter of fact. It is the force that fervently drives the anti-bilingual, English monolingual and monocultural proponents for a return to the "good old days."

Apologetically speaking, the social exercise of excluding "Mexicans" and denying them the same opportunities and equality in American society stems from a white American self-preservation instinct prompted by the conquest of indigenous Mexican territory. For, in effect, in the human drama of war and conquest, and of ethnic and racial self-interest, the ancient western philosophers established some remarkable time-honored long-standing political theories; theories which imperialist leaders of posterity ingested, considered, and practiced. One major tenet was and is that it is politically expedient to keep the indigenous population incorporated by imperialist conquest culturally suppressed and under control.

Conclusively, the political condition being so tense wherein the vanquished and the conqueror share the land side by side; the historical memory and cultural traditions of an indigenous predecessor must be severed for the presumed good of the new social order. A relatively small number of the more brilliant American founding fathers possessed a profound understanding of the ideal prerequisites for a stable secular state. Consequently, it is, therefore, not unreasonable to presume they recognized that a plan had to be devised for the indigenous peoples whose land they coveted and eventually conquered.[92]

For the founding fathers to apply ideas that were developed over the centuries from basic ancient theories was not unrealistic. Thus, the conquest of coveted Mexican territories set the stage for an Anglo-American Mexicanphobia and its subsequent anti-Mexican social ethic. The underlying unspoken fear that in the future the indigenous "Mexican" group might reassert itself in order to reclaim its legacy is an ever-present potential threat to many white Americans. The sentiment is punctuated by the fact the United States government permitted and practiced an apartheid policy against the Mexicans for over one hundred years. A critical issue has been white America's refusal to share

---

92. Most white Americans and their disciples are unaware that the indigenous Native Americans and the Mexican Americans are biologically related. The obvious difference is the manner by which Spanish-speaking and English-speaking imperialists treated the indigenous peoples. The Spanish, like the Romans before them, shared their culture, language institutions, religion, and mixed with the native peoples. The Anglo-Americans did not willingly share any of these things with the Native Americans.

equally with Mexican Americans the country's democratic institutions of freedom, agreed to and bound by treaty with Mexico. Ergo, the governing interests of the now established social order are bent on countering wherever and whenever necessary the Anglo-American anti-thesis—indigenous Hispano-Mexicanism—by disseminating public information in a monocultural way. The naive assumption being that the strategy of denying the one group for the good of the other is aimed at nurturing patriotism; not anything else.

In white southwestern American society a pro-Mexican sentiment is anathema. The design is to present a barren and distorted history of a Hispano-Mexican predecessor, intended to keep the descendants of the conquered race intellectually and psychologically suppressed and unaware. Historically, anti-Hispano-Mexican impulses and thought forms have been impressed early in children's thinking and emotional processes for maximum results.

In review the questions emerge, "is it axiomatic that a state, a body politic stewardship has the authority to usurp the natural rights of a minority to do whatever it judges to be for the good of the whole? Does it possess the moral right to distort history, to misinform or disinform, as well as to repress information, simply because it controls the means to an end?" Within white American elitist circles, notions of freedom and of civil authority, of the desired ends, justifies any means. But the citizenry should be wary because corruption inevitably sets in when institutions are permitted to exercise unchallenged political control.

The historical past has taught humanity that taking a detached intellectual stance sanctions moral apostasy. Surely, elitists and nativists may sincerely believe promoting psychological apartheid and institutionalized racism for the good of the whole is democracy and good. Then, logically it means that training the loyal many without minority debate is presumed to be an acceptable necessary evil for the good of the white status quo, which is the majority of the whole. Regardless, it promotes tyranny by the very fact that it denies the oppressed minority its natural right "to be."

The making and nurturing of the brown American mind and character can best be comprehended in light of the social milieu narrated above. Few Americans of any racial heritage, for example, are fully cognizant that the government violated many of the article guarantees made to the Mexicans in the Treaty of Guadalupe Hidalgo of 1848. Moreover, in American history the causes for the war with Mexico are enshrouded in a *Beowulf-like Manifest Destiny* myth. The American story that the United States paid for the Southwest and California is affixed in the American ethos as a righteous American crusade to the Pacific. Accordingly, following the conquest of Mexican territories by the white Americans, Mexican guerrilla and civil rights champions were labeled bandits. And in the early twentieth century Chicano labor advocates, leaders, and activists were readily outcast as communist troublemakers. This clever delegation to social inferiority facilitates presenting successful and high profile Spanish surnamed socially accommodating brown Americans as "Spanish," or as "Spanish Americans." Denying the brown American community meritorious American status and equality and, thereby, its own brown American leadership is the goal.

Anyway, a "good Mexican" in the southwestern American ethos, is expected to accept second-class citizenship and should be one who does not reprove society's ascribed, however false, Spanish or Hispanic appellation. Furthermore, a "good Mexican" is expected to refrain from asserting or demanding his constitutional rights. A brown American, therefore, is not expected or encouraged to protest either unfair treatment, or the lack of equal opportunity like a white American. Nor is he or she supposed to mobilize and organize like other Americans, to oppose injustices directed at his or her brown compatriots. Responsible and acceptable behavior for a colored minority in respectable American society is ultimate deference to whites. In this connection, it has long been socially determined in the Southwest that Mexicans have a delegated inferior place.

Since, in fact, established time-honored social patterns and social mandates are reinforced by unbroken historical sequences, cultivating public or private negative images of Chicanos and Mexicans continues wherever permitted; unchecked in much of the Southwest. Allegations by Chicanos that Mexican Americans are recognized only when they do something wrong is not without substantial foundation. The Pachuco riots that occurred during World War II is the primary classic example; a remarkable exposé' of a plot in the post-World War II Southwest to reconvert the Chicano population to its pre-war social posture or place is but a close second.

Essentially the latter conspiracy was exposed by a news reporter. It "aimed at depriving Mexican Americans of the few economic and social gains they won during the war." The major goal was to restore the segregated, underpaid, uneducated pool of "Mexican" brown cheap labor that south Texas has always sought to maintain. The "campaign in which the authorities, business and the newspapers all played" their part, "amounted to a conspiracy." Central to the campaign was the trumpeting, or playing up, of a so-called "Mexican" wave of crime and rape; and, demanding sterner repressive action in cases involving "Mexicans." While, "little or no publicity" was given to cases in which Anglos assaulted Mexicans.[93]

Daniel L. Schorr, then news editor of the Netherland News Agency, wrote that little mention was made in Texas newspapers of the incident surrounding the assault on Staff Sergeant Macario Garcia, a Congressional Medal of Honor winner, whose insistence to be served in a cafe prompted the assault in a place where "Mexicans" were not served. Less was known of the case involving Sergeant Jose Mendoza Lopez, also a Medal of Honor hero, who was "thrown out of a restaurant in a small town in the Rio Grande Valley."

Mendoza Lopez was a hero of the Normandy breakthrough, the fierce hedgerow fighting near Saint Lo, France, and Krinkelt, Belgium, where he earned the "distinction of having killed more enemy soldiers (over a hundred Germans) in one action than any other American in the European or Pacific Theaters in World War II." The situation was serious enough for Schorr to write:

> During the war, Texas bigotry and economic discrimination fought a
> holding action. Now a counter offensive is taking shape to wrest from
> the Mexican Americans their economic and social gains. But bitter-
> ness at this "reconversion" is growing and will not long be contained.[94]

---

93. This practice was intended to empower the white community and to sanction discrimination against Mexicans. See Daniel L. Schorr, "Reconverting Mexican Americans." *The New Republic,* Vol. 13, September 30, 1946, pp. 412–413.

94. Raul Morin, *Among the Valiant,* pp. 166–171. Lopez Mendoza was presented with Mexico's Aztec Eagle Award in 1948. He received little public recognition in his own country, the United States, for his heroics. A real American hero was served and honored by the Mexicans.

Schorr, *Ibid,* p. 413.

After the conquest of Mexico's northern provinces, the government disenfranchised approximately 300,000 Mexican citizens by reclassifying them as "Indians" and relocating many in reservations. Thus, the indigenous population which the U.S. government claimed it recognized as tribes and not on the basis of race, was deprived of citizenship status and of their rights in the exchange. See Frederick E. Hoxie, *Indians in American History* (Arlington Heights, IL, Harlan Davidson, Inc., 1988), p. 133.

Since the "No Justice, No Peace Riots," Los Angeles, California, has seen the formation of a "Latino Coalition" between brown American and Latino immigrants for the first time in the history of the city.

THE POLITICAL REALITIES OF BROWN ANGLO-AMERICA

The ongoing major conflict between white and brown Americans has been political power and who will wield it—brown or white Americans. By virtue of superior numbers and by simple exercise of ballot box power brown Americans potentially could politically dominate local politics in hundreds of small communities, and in some cities throughout the Southwest. For this reason, Southwest white Americans, long-time residents in these brown dominated communities, have viewed the voting power potential of the "Mexican" community with alarm. Ergo, a real fear of brown American racial unity and the group's subsequent democratic assumption of political power is germane to the discriminatory tactics used against brown Americans.

To avert what whites view as possible political catastrophe, they have wholeheartedly supported the rigid anti-ethnic policies regimented by educational social custom and tradition. Most knowledgeable whites know the monocultural system splinters and divides minority loyalty and affiliation. Brown American nationalism and any potential for racial unity is, therefore, dashed by design in the schools. For whites to maintain control, therefore, it is imperative that whites and their brown Anglo friends dominate and manage policy-making school boards, the political machinery and higher education. And, also, to determine and control whatever foreign-sounding label they may deem necessary to ascribe to the subordinated brown American community.

Ironically, the systematic general exclusion and unequal sharing of political power in the past, is generating brown American dissidence and activism in the present. Political mechanisms aimed at suppressing political unity portend the very end result power hungry and racist whites fear most; that is, their loss of political power to brown Americans through the ballot box. The harsh internal colony curtain that has kept Chicanos powerless in the Southwest is gradually disintegrating as Chicanos are deculturated and individualized.

Frankly, when brown Americans parallel or surpass the political dissidence and objectifying mentality of the white American status quo, demand for real change will suddenly materialize; for the obvious reason that such has been the American way of other colored minorities in American history! American culture nurtures a strong personal desire to be somebody in the American body politic. It also cultivates dissidence and political empowerment aspirations. Given the realities of

circumstance, surely it is only a matter of time before a brown dissident community massively joins and clamors for equal American status and political participation on a grand scale. Unlike university
student unions, that forthcoming event portends severe socioeconomic
implications.

Governed by this potential premise to avert disaster ahead and
probable general chaos and disorder, drastic and absolute establishment changes are mandated. The Voting Rights Act of 1975 and 1982
set new standards to parry the growing disaffection. Frankly, history
has taught humanity repeatedly that a conjunction of political power
and prosperity is fertile ground for arrogance—the kind of foolishness
that clouds perception and reason. In this callous manner ultra right-
wing and racist status quo whites and others, for example, have confi-
dently adhered to the belief that as in the past any concerted brown
American quest for political empowerment can be deterred.

A hard-hearted egotism blinds many to the impending new reality.
For despite a growing socialist leaning among young Mexican Americans, costly public school boycotts, and other civil disorders throughout the Southwest on through the 1990s, status quo leadership refuses
to focus on the real issues. Tokenism, window dressing, and quota systems are but paltry mechanisms for pacification. They are best
described by critics as "band-aid solutions," because in actuality they
are not intended to solve any deep-rooted or long-term problems. In
truth, they are most particularly counter-productive.

Three neo-Chicano scholars—Mario Barrera, Carlos Munoz, and
Charles Ornelas—have examined the origins and development of the
internal colony in the Southwest as it relates to the barrio. They succinctly delineated what constitutes freedom, and a true solution for Chicano self-determination:

> To be considered an effective solution, a proposed change must con-
> tribute to decolonization—that is, it must enable Chicanos to gain
> greater control over their environment while maintaining their col-
> lective identity. This means among other things, increasing the range
> of alternatives open to Chicanos and developing Chicano control over
> those institutions which most directly affect their lives. Those
> approaches which seek to incorporate Chicanos into Anglo institu-
> tions without making fundamental changes in those institutions will

not contribute to decolonization, although they may allow individual Chicanos to increase their social mobility.[95]

In large metropolitan areas like Los Angeles County, the federal Voters Rights Act has dramatically paved the way for political inclusion of brown Americans and Latinos. With M.A.L.D.E.F.[96] leading the redistricting effort in court, notable political empowerment in city councils, on boards of supervisors, and boards of education has been the result. The potential for greater local empowerment is self-evident in cities like Los Angeles.

However, the fact the system requires judicial redistricting mandates to give Spanish surname Americans a fair chance to get elected, is an undeniable reflection of the region's deep-rooted anti-Hispano-Mexican, anti-Catholic, and anti-brown-skinned (Indian) sentiments. Also, the fact Chicano groups as Americans are utilizing the system to create that necessary political change for leadership opportunities reflects constructive brown American attitudinal political progress.

Creating political conditions to make it possible for Chicanos and Latinos to be electable for the first time in history, by legal redistricting, has been harshly criticized and opposed by white and secular Jewish status quo opponents in large cities like Los Angeles. The reaction and opposition to these changes has been revealing, because it is precisely these groups who collectively have never voted for Chicanos and Latinos regardless of personal qualifications—white Anglos who have possessed the reins of political power since the conquest of California and the Southwest from Mexico. The conquering race has, since the big rape as Chicano scholars refer to it, spared few political mechanisms to deter brown Americans from acquiring political empowerment. Moreover, the growing clamor against widening democratic practices is exposing and laying bare the most threatened racial groups opposed to brown American empowerment, as their fears of losing control in the city of Los Angeles grow.[97]

---

95. Mario Barrera, Carlos Munoz, and Charles Ornelas, "The Barrio as an Internal Colony," in *People and Politics in Urban Society,* Vol. VI of Urban Affairs Annual reviews; ed. by Harlan Hahn (Beverly Hills, CA: Sage Publications, 1972), p. 295

96. MALDEF is an abbreviation for Mexican American Legal Defense and Education Fund.

97. In a city not known or tarnished with a history of anti-semitism (like New York, Boston, or Chicago), but rather one marked with a torrid history of Mexican lynchings, Indian genocide, and an unforgiving anti-Mexican animus and violence, in concert with an ongoing brown American political powerlessness and poverty, the commentary below by Joel Kotkin is most enlightening.

Lamentably that is not all it reveals. As Chicanos and Mexican Americans have begun to establish themselves politically, some seats of government in areas composed of majority or near majority brown American constituencies, common knowledge suggests it should be coveted and held by a person of Mexican descent. In Los Angeles an assembly seat, for example, supposedly a "Latino" seat became an issue because the outgoing assemblyman endorsed a "non-Latino" for that office. Fundamentally, the clamor grew in support of the notion that it should be held by a "Latino" because it had taken brown Americans so long to acquire that the minuscule political power it now held.

Of course, most Americans understand the bloc politics process. Addressing the so-called black vote, the Jewish vote, or the Irish vote by candidates is not approved by many people. But it is the way of American politics. Equally important is that white Americans have held all the political power and have never cared to share it with Chicanos or Mexican Americans. They still control the machinery of government at all levels of interchange.

White Anglo Americans rarely vote or elect brown American candidates regardless of their qualifications. Americans with names like Sanchez, Lopez, Martinez, Juarez, and Gomez have little chance of gaining high powered political office without big party support. For brown Americans, then, to espouse to hold on to the few gains they have made in nearly fifty years of significant effort is understandable. Nonetheless, when brown Americans exercise bloc voting techniques like other Americans they are accused of being ethnocentric or of being politically immature by the ignorant and bigoted.

Kotkin wrote that in Los Angeles the Jews are the "most prominent and influential white authority in the city." And that, "[if] faced with the prospect of living in a THIRD WORLD CITY (emphasis mine) ruled by racial and political radicals many Jews—their concerns ignored, their lives and businesses threatened, vilified as exploiters—would feel compelled to leave." See *The Los Angeles Times,* July 26, 1992.

In their quest to retain their long enjoyed vast political power, Jews are implicated by association. This scenario strongly suggests the Jews in Aztlan must recognize they have been part of the anti-Mexican problem, clearly in collusion with vile Anglo-American interests. Jews threaten litigation, legislation, changing election, and judicial rules with the finite purpose of retarding democracy for brown Americans. Actions prompted by imagined fears or racist attitudes of having to share political power with their brown American neighbors.

Such has been their response to the redistricting effort of the Los Angeles School Board of Education by Chicanos and Latinos, whose children compose over 70% of the student body in the district, whose astronomical dropout rate breeds violent gang warfare and terror in their communities. See *The Los Angeles Times,* August 2, 1992, and the *Los Angeles Daily News,* July 14, 1992.

CHAPTER 12

The Internal Colony Labyrinth:

Non-Colonized, Non-Chicano Roles

*I*t is superfluous to stress how the original design of the internal colony was intended to nurture the inferior and confused brown Anglo-Saxon Protestant typology, and the socially dysfunctional character of the Mexican American; types preferred by the establishment to help them control the more colonized and less *agabachado* Chicano population. Therefore, for "Mexican leadership" to be valid and credible in the eyes of the white or brown Anglo ally, it must stem from this individualized self-centered typology—in other words, from among brown characters who are at least psychologically nearly Anglo.

Community oriented brown leaders whose purpose and design proposes to uplift the socioeconomic status or awareness of Chicanos in the barrios, are unabashedly labeled irresponsible un-American agitators and radicals. Grassroots activism is viewed with suspicion on the false presumption it is subversive, because it proposes to help Chicanos help themselves as Chicanos. Detached and indifferent sentiments to personal ethnicity or race are considered desirable and acceptable "leadership" traits for minorities by white American managers. Whites are the norm and whites set the standards in all areas of endeavor, particularly in politics.

The majority group elite persistently maintains by inference, example and in writing, that Chicanos must acquiesce to a fixed, however functional, white superiority to be acceptable Americans. Therefore, a Chicano's identity is made dependent on the white American's whims. Equal representation and political opportunity are more difficult goals for a brown American to realize; simply because all the prerequisites for elitist brown leadership that excludes most sensitized barrio activists, were set many decades ago. Perverted self-interest and veiled paranoia still motivates the status quo to press for complete assurance that a brown American leader be free of minority anguish.[98]

Brown American leaders are eternally encouraged and expected to affirm they will help solve the problems of the entire community and not just exclusively the "Mexican" community. This special qualification burdens Chicanos because this additional requirement is leveled only on brown American leaders. In actuality it is camouflaged racism. In the past, brown Americans were expected and often required to prove they were "professional Mexicans" to be acceptable to whites. In other words, to be non-colonized, non-Chicanos with all that it entails—only brown Anglo-Saxon Protestants need apply.

In this regard social scientists and others should appreciate what is fundamentally at the root of white Americans' delight in hearing Mexican Americans assert they are whites, when in fact they are not. Equally gratifying to dominant group sensitivities are responses by reasonable Mexican American leaders, or acculturated-deculturated celebrities of Mexican origin, who are appointed or elected to public office or posts, make public avowals that they "will serve all the people regardless of ethnic, racial or national origin without distinction." Indeed, it must be more laudable and joyous to the Caucasian ear to hear self-made personalities like Lee Trevino, the golfer, allege that he is "not an ethnic group," and reject an offer to aid anguished minorities against racist practices by boycotting a golf event.[99]

Yet, to hear Reies Tijerina decry injustices perpetrated upon Chicanos in the Southwest, even though his words echo the patriotism of Patrick Henry, is an anathema. Professional athletes play to win and to enrich themselves. Therefore, interrogation of a personality like Trevino as to whether he is "playing and winning for his people" because his people are presumed to be Chicanos is masked racism. The

---

98. Minority anguish that is born and nourished by racism, social exclusion, deprivation of a positive self-esteem, and pride in being an American of Mexican descent.

99. *Los Angeles Times,* September 27, 1972.

obviously ethnic-loaded questions hide the true motive. They are more truly intended to determine whether Trevino is a "professional Mexican," or just another ethnically anguished Chicano.

For the historical record, Trevino, in fact, stated that he "disassociates himself from political movements, especially those with a Mexican American complexion" because as he put it, "I don't believe in helping just one race or nationality . . . I'm only concerned with the poor, white, yellow, red—and the youth [Chicanos?] . . . I don't want to segregate. That's exactly backwards."[100] The logical conclusion is that Trevino is a "professional Mexican." Trevino's remarks, after making the "big time," that he used "to be Mexkin [sic], but I'm making money now so I'm gonna be a Spaniard" evidently was not offered as a joke. These are examples of counter ethnic mind-set or mental attitudes shared by majority group persons. That they are impressed on the brown American for the various aforementioned reasons requires no further elaboration.

Chicanos are discouraged from expressing and developing empathy and cohesion for their own ethnic group by systematic differential socialization, individualization, and deculturation. Purposefully this process cultivates the social dynamics of southwestern American life, but via the internal colony. Thus, the often heard allegation that ethnic empathy, assertiveness, and pride promotes separatism is absurd; since, in fact, it is the monocultural differential socialization practice of dividing minority groups that has spawned the separatism that currently prevails.

Multicultural structuring an educational and social environment in which Chicanos and other browns—as well as blacks, Native Americans, and Asians—can celebrate themselves for what they are strengthens, not weakens, American culture for the ultimate good of the whole. The range of freedom encompasses the totality of humanity. A person's ethnic or racial identity is the subjective and objective self by definition, respectively. To vent that individuality and self-identity is a fundamental right of American freedom. Individual freedom and modern philosophy were born and developed on the premise and method of "knowing thyself," an ideal synthesized by Socrates more than two millenniums past.

---

100. *Sports Illustrated,* December 20, 1971, p. 39. *Los Angeles Examiner,* January 6, 1971.

Conversely, "false" Americanization and monoculturalism are freedom limiting processes because they inhibit colored Americans from expressing their colored Americanness. On the contrary, it demands uncompromising cultural and spiritual alienation; it encourages an aversion for the Mexican heritage. Despite this, it is a highly lauded process, although it causes socially dysfunctional colored American personalities. For example, deferring to the supposedly more naturally endowed and racially superior white Americans, brown Americans are also expected to denigrate, and when among whites, to shun persons of Mexican background in order to demonstrate an absence of lower ethnic affinity. But while most whites realize that brown Americans can never be exactly like them, principally white, it is expected that they should make the impossible effort anyway. How did that old Nazi rhyme go? "Ein folk, ein reich, ein . . ."

BEHIND PALLID MASKS: REAL CHICANO IMAGES

Status and image are two highly prized human characteristics in most societies. In the United States maintaining the "good" name of a business, an educational institution, a religious denomination, or a university athletic status go hand in hand. It is critically important in many social circles that we belong to the right church, attend or have attended the right college, that we have a high status position, that we associate in the proper social circles, and that we are members of the right race, or have the right national origin.

Numerous favored traits will ad literum make us or break us in American society. To be of Mexican descent represents a trait that automatically excludes most brown persons from any possible right association or connections. Mexicanphobia and odium for La Raza in the Southwest, inclusive even of persons with a blue-blood Spanish heritage, is much too formidable in the American ethos to secure a white or full-blooded American status.

It is common knowledge among foreign visitors to the United States that most white Americans are uncommonly ignorant not only of the histories of foreign countries, but of their very own history. Aside from prominent names like George Washington, Abraham Lincoln, Robert E. Lee, Theodore Roosevelt, John F. Kennedy, and certain great events, a true knowledge of American history is lacking among most Americans surveys show. Inextricably, where history fades folklore ascends.

Anglo-American folklore is so synergized with factual history that most Americans find it difficult to distinguish between the two. Thus, the "discovery" of America by Cristóbal Colón (Columbus in English) and the Santa María is associated with the founding of Jamestown and the Mayflower. The battle of the Alamo, a Mexican event, has become an American national shrine and so the story goes. The historical mix of fantasy and sentiment ingrained in the Anglo-American mind was incorporated from old British traditions. American civilization simply acquired old British enemies, inclusive of the eternal rejection of Spain and Spanish surnamed personages, and added its own. Consequently, unless the peculiar mixture of American history and folklore is modified, the brown or Spanish surnamed American will continue to be seen and treated as an adverse alien fact in American culture.

When whites presume superiority over "Mexicans," they conduct themselves according to expected social custom. Within certain social circles in the Southwest a culturally innate white-American sentiment to play out the role of superiority is the norm; a vile practice which still engenders considerable conflict between the two groups. Brown Americans are most culpable because they consent to the will, guidance, or suggestion of whites, for no other sound reason than having been socially conditioned to do so during their formative years. Indeed, as a prominent Mexican American once wrote:

> There is a common belief among Mexican Americans that in order to get equal opportunity you must be better than your majority counterpart. It is also commonly accepted that in order to receive higher recognition you must be the best. The Mexican American believes this and not without justification.[101]

Frankly, anyone can feel uncomfortable if certain expectations are not met. That is surely the case with the social expectations learned in school and reinforced by social custom.

---

101. Armando V. Rodriguez, former president of East Los Angeles College. Rodriguez immigrated to the United States after his formative years. He was not a Chicano. Yet, he became the first person of Mexican ancestry to be elevated to a community college presidency in the history of California higher education. Ironically, he was inaugurated by then Los Angeles College Chancellor, Leslie Koital, a Jewish-Hungarian refugee.

BROWN AMERICAN MEXICAN ANTIPATHIES

Brown Americans find themselves in a unique quandary in the Southwest. White Americans reject them as full-fledged citizens, and Mexicans refer to them derogatorily as *pochos* and *agringados* (faded Mexicans and gringo-like). Yet, while in all candor, Mexicans may be justified for distrusting Mexican Americans given the historical sequences of the past, many Mexicans do not conceal their contempt and dislike for the gringo "brown copies" of the United States.

Furthermore, it is not particularly surprising to discover that Mexicans hold brown Americans sometimes in greater contempt than they do white Americans. A growing number of brown Americans speak only English, possess little knowledge of Mexico and the Mexican people, and like most white Americans, tend to regard Mexicans as their social inferiors. Consequently, considerable subtle contempt festers between Mexicans, Chicanos, and the more *agabachado* deculturated marginal brown Americans in the American Southwest.

In historical retrospect, it was the Mexican Americans who drew first blood by their vile behavior toward Mexican immigrants between 1910 and 1940. That action generated the ill will and reciprocal dislike among Mexican immigrants and visitors. The enmity between the earlier settlers and the more recent immigrants and their descendants constitutes a negative self-evident legacy in Aztlan. Civil war in Mexico, including the 1910 Revolution and the Cristero Rebellion in the 1920s, displaced thousands of miserably poor *peones* and *campesinos.* Hundreds of thousands fled north to the United States.[102]

Mexican Americans, like other Americans, were not the most cordial hosts as they, in their defensive posture of being singled out for discrimination, took on a superior stance. Thus, the result was to denigrate the impoverished Mexican refugees by all form of vile behavior and demeaning and offensive labels. Mexican Americans, for example, referred to Mexican immigrants as *chuntaros* (stupid Mexican national), *cholos* (low-class Indian), *zurumatos* (dummies), *patas rajadas* (scared feet), and *guaras* (abbreviation for *guaraches* [sandals]).

---

102. President Woodrow Wilson's Mexican policy permitting Mexican rebels to purchase weapons in the United States to overthrow the constitutional government of Mexico's Victorian Huerta was the catalyst and source of the 1910 Revolution. See John Latham, Woodrow Wilson's Foreign Policy.

The Mexicans reciprocated with the *Pocho* (faded Mexican) and *agringado* (gringo-like) labels. The latter appellations still connote ethnic betrayal and biting contempt. Moreover, the term, *agringado,* is highly disparaging because in Mexican usage it refers to an Anglo-American-like brown person. One might ask: what is wrong with that? Evidently not too much, unless you behave like what in popular Mexican thought is perceived as a contemptible anti-Mexican white American.

Remarkably, *Pochos* are as contemptible to Mexicans as *vendidos* (sell-outs) are to Chicanos. Because of social circumstances the fact remains that Chicanos are neither culturally Anglo-American or Mexican. Chicanos can most correctly be described and defined as a distinctive ethnic, group. In this regard, the Mexican observer quite justifiably considers himself socially superior to the *Pocho* because the latter is a culturally alienated ethnic composite. And, moreover, *pochos* are invariably ashamed of their ancestry. Mexicans, consequently, have stigmatized all brown Americans as *Pochos* since the beginning of the second half of the twentieth century. Therefore, in a generic sense, at least, all brown Americans regardless of how culturally Mexican they may be are potential *Pochos* to most Mexicans.

Regrettably, most Mexican nationals are actually oblivious to the causes that nurture the brown Americans' negative view of Mexicans as a people. The deculturation, aversion to being Mexican conditioning, and the anti-Mexican training and influence of American public school socialization and society, as the origins for their antipathies toward Mexicans, escapes even the brown Americans themselves. For, frankly, to many brown Americans, Mexican nationals are foreign objects with the universal stigma of social inferiority that is common to all foreigners in all the nations of the world.

In the United States all students regardless of race are mass-programmed and institutionalized in a remarkably standard way. Therefore, an ethnic sense of anti-Mexicanism is an American way of life mode learned by all students, including many Chicanos; some of whom learn their anti-Mexican lessons only too well. In this connection, the dynamics in the making of the Chicano mind requires a closer examination of generally and purposefully ignored, or overlooked, distinctions between Mexican nationals and brown Americans.

Whether it is diffused awareness or focused consciousness, and despite the obvious national, cultural, and behavioral realities, neo-Chicano intellectual visionaries for a variety of unsound reasons abhor making any distinction between brown Americans and Mexican nationals. In other words, they must have it in their own erroneous and ambiguous way in order to achieve a semblance of nationalist unity or, perhaps, to cover their ulterior political motives. This ambiguous posturing is preferable to them rather than the reality that the commonality between Mexicans and Chicanos is not necessarily culture, but race. Like, let us say, between Germans and Americans of German descent, or Italians and Americans of Italian descent. All people with a common denominator—race.

Most Central Americans are of the same indigenous race as persons of Mexican ancestry. And, they most certainly are not Mexicans. The situation is comparable to white Americans and Europeans. They belong to the same race or stock but Americans are not Europeans, and the latter are not Americans. However, this portends that when brown Americans of Mexican and Latin American descent become aware of their common racial bond, political unity could more probably be forged under a racial banner.

For the record, it is not too far-fetched to expect that alliances in the future between the *indios del sur* (indigenous Mexican peoples) and the *indios del norte* form the United States reservations, will also eventually come to pass.[103] But, a gnawing question emerges. If Chicanos are not Mexicans, and a *mestizo* does not constitute a Mexican, then what should a person believe? The answer is simple: Chicanos are descendant, for the most part, from the *indios del sur* who were the original peoples of pre-Hispanic tribal Mexico. The massive host indigenous group did not suddenly disappear into some absurd *mestizaje* abyss or new race, but rather it absorbed those Spaniards who intermingled with them. In the northward Hispano-Mexican movement that followed Apaches, Pimas, Chumash, Yumas, and others also racially mingled with the *indios del sur.*

---

103. The *indios del norte* in this case are those persons of indigenous American ancestry who are tribe or Indian nation affiliated or in reservations. It does not include the known and unknown millions of white and black Americans of mixed Indian ancestry.

Between 15% and 18% of Mexico's population, according to Mexican census tabulators is white. The remainder is unmixed indigenous or slightly mixed non-white.

CHAPTER 13

Those Mexicans:

A Republican Protestant View

For generations Americans have been offered narrow one-sided Black Legend-like accounts of Mexican history and Mexican character by a grossly insensitive and hostile elite intelligentsia. Decades of inaccurate, unkind, and antagonistic narratives, both fiction and non-fiction, regarding the race, religion, and culture of Mexico by the ivory tower and its disciples have, in effect, negatively impacted American thought and culture in reference to the Mexican. Distorted expositions and dishonest presentations have made persons of Mexican descent, unlike descendants of Europeans, distinctively the most foreign and anti-American elements in Anglo-American folklore, and in the real-life situations of the United States.

Francisco Armando Rios, an English professor, poignantly painted American society's conceptualization of the Mexican with the following notation:

> Popular American usage does not expressly distinguish between the Mexican national and American-born citizens of more or less remote Mexican ancestry. The popular imagination mixed them both into a stereotype that is at once quaint and threatening. Across the length of the United States, the symbol of the Mexican is the peon, asleep against the wall of his adobe hut or at the foot of the saguaro cactus. At best he wears only sandals. He is lazy and given to putting things off until *mañana*. This picturesque fellow and his inevitable burro

adorn the menus and neon signs of restaurants and motels across the U.S. At some point in his life the peon wakes up, takes a drink of tequila, puts on his wide-brimmed sombrero, and emigrates to the United States—by swimming the Rio Grande, of course. Once here, he loses his picturesque and harmless ways and becomes sinister: he is now proud and hot-blooded, easily offended, intensely jealous, a drinker, a brawler, a knifer, cruel, promiscuous, a flashy dresser, a good dancer, and depending on the judge, a "Latin lover" or a "lousy lover."[104]

The Mexican and the brown American have been anathematized in Anglo-American letters by this form of insidious racist hate humor. Since, in fact, all Spanish-surnamed brown Americans are presumed to be Mexicans, then, the stereotypes are also applicable to them. If the student of the Chicano mind and character can fathom this truth, then, he will have taken the first step toward a better understanding of the institutionalized inferior status of the brown American, and, perhaps come to understand the basis for the lower class status in the cultural milieu of the United States of Mexicanness. Academe has led the way, the so-called cutting edge, in deluding and patterning American society in its negative stereotypical Mexican characterization.

Ergo, a paucity of scholarly materials and publications on the accomplishments and contributions to American life by Mexicans and brown Americans, is indicative of more than coincidental omission. A time-honored design to suppress, and to extinguish any credible memory and awareness to any precedent society to American civilization among Americans in the Southwest, gathers considerable support here given the evidence. While at first glance it may even appear to be institutionalized myopia, careful review points to a well-formed politically grounded plan.

Surely under careful scrutiny any given notion that the major goal for omissions of this order are intended to protect the white Anglo-Saxon American Way, is self-evident. To guard against critical honest assessment, insignificant or scant attention is given to either current or past Spanish surnamed American personalities and heroes. A true basis for fear of comparative analysis, which could lead to rendering equality to non-whites, is a primary concern. For this reason Americans of all races rarely see successful or beautiful brown American images or

---

104. Octavio Romano, ed., *Voices* (Berkeley: Quinto Sol Publications, 1971), pp. 60–61.

heroes. In the great majority of cases whites are showcased as achievers or as models of success by the media and the schools. Notably, in this manner, "Mexican" inferiority and white American superiority positions are respectively strengthened and perpetuated.[105]

BROWN AMERICANS OR MEXICANS?

Sociologists point out that any citizen of the United States who has been mass-educated (some prefer to call it institutionalized) in America's public schools will learn socially acceptable prejudices and biases regarding ethnics or racial groups. Two sociologists, George E. Simpson and J. Milton Yinger, analyzed this phenomenon below:

> We learn these cultural responses in the same way that we acquire other attitudes and behavior patterns. Belief in the superiority of the Caucasian race is as natural to the average white American as is belief in monogamy or knowledge of the correct way to dress. The speech and action of those around him, his observation of status differentials among the races, the joke she hears, the histories he reads, the rewards and punishments he receives for various actions toward members of minority groups all teach him the correct behavior as it is defined by his society. He does not have to have an individual experience with members of minority groups; he will often be equipped with ready-made responses in advance of any such experience, or even in the complete absence of contact.[106]

The enduring image of the brown American, even in high official circles, as foreign-like and un-American is the result of callous ignorance because this observation is stereotypically based. In other words, the brown American is categorized by an identifiable skin color or Spanish surname as un-American.

A very public and good example of this culturally ingrained predisposition and practice occurred on September 4, 1964, when the late Lyndon Baines Johnson appointed Raul Castro, a Tucson Arizona

---

105. Television commercials are a classic example of discrimination via omission. Rarely are brown American people presented in commercials although in some major cities like Los Angeles, California, and San Antonio, and El Paso, Texas, they represent over half or nearly half the population of potential consumers.

106. George E. Simpson and J. Milton Yinger, *Racial and Cultural Minorities: An Analysis of Prejudice and Discrimination* (New York; Harper and Bros., 1964), p. 67.

Superior Court Judge, Ambassador to El Salvador. The appointment was unique in American politics leading *Time Magazine* to focus on the supposed un-American racial and ethnic character of Castro's surname by writing:

> CASTRO SI, YANQUI SI: Names like Cabot and MacArthur are certainly American. Even Labouisse and Poullada or Reinhardt and Riddleberger do not seem very out of place on the roster of U.S. ambassadors, but the newest name in the diplomatic ranks will have them haggling. Last week President Johnson appointed as U.S. Ambassador to El Salvador a man named Raul Castro . . . To knock the U.S. now, leftist Salvadorans will also have to knock Castro [Cuba].[107]

On April 28, 1967, *Time Magazine* published an article entitled "Pocho's Progress," which, is safe to say, still lingers as the level of understanding and acceptance educated Americans have of brown Americans. The article mindlessly described Mexican Americans as *pochos, cholos, pachucos, machos, agringados,* and the United States as supposedly conceived by brown Americans, as *gringolandia.*

The brown American community leadership was outraged. Congressman Edward R. Roybal, a Hispano, demanded before Congress that *Time Magazine* "issue an immediate apology for gratuitous affront and calculated ethnic slur against the Spanish-speaking community of our southwestern states."[108] The honorable Roybal was accurate in his assessment of the slighting of Chicanos when he stated before Congress:

> The article is replete with the kind of coded, but easily identified ethnic slurs well-calculated to stir latent prejudice in an unsuspecting reader—a regrettable example of a vicious type of free-wheeling journalistic license unworthy of the high standard of factual reporting we have a right to expect from any reputable magazine . . . The bigotry and bias of the writer is clearly evidenced in the article . . . and is an affront and insult to persons of Mexican descent in both Mexico and the United States.[109]

Shortly afterwards Roybal, who would have been expected to pursue the matter more vigorously, was asked in Los Angeles if he really

---

107. *Time Magazine,* September 5, 1964.

108. *Los Angeles Times,* May 12, 1967.

109. *Congressional Record,* Vol. CVIII, May 2, 1967.

expected an apology. He was quoted as saying, "Not really . . . it's a matter of educating them."[110] Indeed, while Roybal had stood up well in publically defending La Raza, he had not yet learned to "bite." For on the same day that the honorable Roybal made the above statement, *Time Magazine* used the term *pocho* a second time in reference to the federal appointment of Armando Rodriguez as coordinator of the new Mexican American Affairs Unit of the United States Office of Education![111]

CHICANISMO, THE BEST OF TWO CULTURES: TRUE ASSIMILATION

Doubtless a closer examination of the social cleavage among brown Anglo-Saxon republican Protestants, Mexican immigrants, and barrio Chicanos should expand our understanding regarding the group's socioeconomic trends. The less economically fortunate Chicanos, for example, are commonly criticized by all groups for being lazy and caught up in their own ethos. Most whites, the more materially successful brown Americans, and the psychologically sound and proud Mexican immigrant, are unable to fathom the crisis of identity and lack of self-worth impressed on the Chicano psyche by a hostile monocultural Anglo-American school social environment. This is the origin of the former being "caught up in their own ethos"; the state of mind preferred for them by the establishment.

Guiding brown Americans into this energy-wasting and uninventive cycle or state of mind exculpates those responsible for the poverty and social problems of the Chicano community itself. On top of this, a paucity of research and information encourages the forging of false premises that invariably lead to incredibly misguided allegations. The brown American community, one classic hostile Anglo theory goes, harbors little ambition and desire for progress. Failure and lack of achievement, alleges another, is nurtured in uncaring and educationally insensitive family settings.[112]

---

110. *Los Angeles Times,* May 12, 1967.

111. *Time Magazine,* May 12, 1967.

112. Non-Chicano Spanish surname persons who appear to speak with authority, like ex-Secretary of Education Lauro Cavazos, who on more than one occasion chastised Spanish surname parents for not doing more to help their youngsters attain educationally. Also, see Chavez, *Out of the Barrio,* pp. 168–169. Moreover, antagonist brown Anglo feminists with little or no stake in the brown American community, charge that Chicano and Mexican values that encourage marriage and motherhood roles exact a brain drain among brown women. The inference is that it also holds back brown men.

Popular and offensive unscientific conclusions of this nature echo the defunct racial credos of the Social Darwinists, who in their misguided doctrine measured the causes of poverty in the United States by racial and cultural determinist standards alone. Brown and black Americans, it was suggested, had only themselves to blame for their wretched socioeconomic condition. Successful and assertive individuals were smart. The dumb and lazy fell by the wayside. In this intellectual theoretical sway, material gain, and its pervasive influence, were presumed to be the cardinal indicators of an individual's superior intelligence and human worth.

Thus, traditional value systems which espoused human sensitivity, good social breeding, including a respectable family, human dignity, good manners, and morals were adjudged to be a false philosophy of life. White American secularism and its type of self-centered personality formation requires that the latter be superseded by a narcissistic secular humanism and a capitalist conceptualization of class based on wealth and material value. Many native-born brown Americans, expectedly, have been influenced by this point of reference; ergo, the brown Anglos and the Aspirants described in this study. And frankly, many of the most assertive brown Americans have failed to succeed materially. Not usually for lack of effort, but fundamentally due to discrimination and racism.

Since "Mexicans" in the American ethos are rated very low socially (i.e., poor and un-American), theoretically for Mexican Americans to undergo significant socioeconomic mobility they must first discard their Mexican and Chicano character and imitate the majority, i.e., the white Anglo-American.[113] Whereby, a marked psychological apartheid emerged as the established pattern and a way of life for those who unknowingly or consciously lose their freedom "to be."

Besides, the much-lauded supposition that the supremacist melting pot process works, rather than the more realistic admission that it does not, is popularized by the overblown success of a few "Mexicans"; thus, the lauded pervasive stance that a Chicano must shed his Mexicanness in order to uplift himself materially and socially. The brown American who resists by retaining a semblance of his Mexicanness, i.e., being

---

113. Mexicans and Chicanos cannot assimilate and disappear because they, like other non-whites, are color visible. So becoming like Anglos (whites) does not make them any less "Mexican" looking.

Chicano, discovers that his proud and autonomous self-image is viewed as a handicap by many racist Americans and culturally alienated brown people.

Yet, in all practicality, most Mexicans and brown Americans are beyond redemption or regeneration to those very same critics. For even if Mexican Americans could realistically cast off their social and psychological "foreignness," they remain Mexicans, or Latinos, or Hispanics, in popular thinking. In the white American ethos the Mexicans' identification, like among other colored peoples, is riveted on race. Brown Americans are distinctive and identifiable because they are a colored minority in a white dominated United States.

Nonetheless, assimilating the best elements of two cultures is a less popular alternative among white Americans. Remarkably, the irony is that Chicanismo is the by-product composite or synthesis of the two clashing cultures. True cultural assimilation requires, in fact, a two-way forging. But whites are monocultural and monolingual oriented and have every intention of remaining that way. Yet, besides that obstinate posture, brown Americans generally are committed to the idea that Mexican Americans can survive by "taking the best of each culture and coming out with an unbeatable combination."

In the Southwest and California the Spanish language is rejected as co-equal with English. If the steadfast reluctance of the majority to learn Spanish reveals anything, real assimilation is impossible so long as a cultural one-way street persists in the old Aztlan. Be that as it may, Chicanismo while being a real cultural synthesis or blend is unattractive to white Americans and highly marginalized brown Americans. Given the supremacist stance of the melting pot ideal that has nurtured American minds, there is absolutely no way it could be acceptable. So, despite the time-honored fact that it is a mentally healthy cultural composite for brown Americans, assimilation, arguably, is not, and has never been a sought after American societal goal in the Southwest. Nor has it either with black Americans or Native Americans in any other region on the North American continent.

Rather, "false" Americanization, monoculturalism, and individualism have the finite purpose of keeping the non-white communities divided, isolated, and seething under wraps with dangerous and odious feelings; in addition to the more recent psycho-sociological and economic dependency on majority group approbation. The predictable by-product is an organism gripped and guided by an endless psychological

antagonism that succeeds in a result of a narrow monocultural supremacist secular humanism gone awry in a democratic society. This same
process, in short, is the seat of most of the social problems encountered
by brown Americans; it fuels and fans counter-cultural Chicanismo.

In all sincerity, given this extraordinary scenario, how is a libertarian and freethinking person supposed to reconcile the American doctrine that espouses the "dignity of each man, woman and child—and
the special right each individual possesses to make his own decisions
and lead his own life," with uncompromising ethnocide, the social differentiation, social isolation, and economic deprivation of the Chicano
reality?

SECOND-CLASS CITIZENSHIP

When brown Americans collectively challenge white society's expectations of them, such as demanding to be called Chicanos instead of
Mexicans, a veiled degree of hostility is reflected in deprecation of such
a plan, or at best Caucasians accept it almost with a sense of mirth.
Whites prefer to maintain a friendly domination of Chicanos, not only
in their minds, but in the totality of human affairs. Evidence to support this contention can be found in the numerous Chicano Studies
programs established in the intellectual soil of higher education campuses throughout the Southwest during the late 1960s. Few of these
programs were ever economically controlled by Chicanos.[114] Thus,
while not rigidly authoritarian unless challenged, racist white American
bureaucrats maintain shaky control bedded in mingled ear and contempt.

A major cause for incompatible police–Chicano community relations is historically rooted in widespread ignorance. Many police officers view brown Americans as foreigners rather than as compatriots to
be protected. Epitaphs like *pancho, pachuco,* dirty Mexican, beaner,
taco, niggers, and stupid Mexican, are of common enough usage
among white policemen to suggest little sensitivity exists among their
ranks. Presumed to be socially inferior and devoid of civil rights, Chicanos are often accorded the treatment of second-class citizens by

---

114. Economic and major leadership roles are similarly restricted to whites among protestant
proselytizing groups, regardless of the merits and training of the brown American member pros-
elytizers.

policemen. Frankly, it is common knowledge in the brown community and a well substantiated fact in academe that European and other white foreigners are accorded better treatment than Chicano citizens.

Brown American community efforts to correct these injustices are generally denounced by white and B.A.S.P. oppressors as divisive, and as threats to American institutions. The brown community subsequently finds itself in a quandary. Brown people live in a free land but are unable to successfully secure freedom from police harassment and excessive use of force. The publicized videotaped Rodney King case beating in Los Angeles, California, in 1991 led to an investigation of the Los Angeles Police Department. The resulting Warren Christopher Report recommended reforms in the police department, including new policies regarding the use of excessive use of force in the colored minority communities.[115]

While it may be expected by some that police irregularities will occur because of the generally lower educational attainment of policemen as compared to, for example, judges, the evidence strongly suggests that such is not always the case. On September 2, 1969, for example, Judge Gerald S. Chargin of San Jose, California, made national news by reprimanding a young Chicano accused of incest with the suggestion that he "ought to commit suicide," and by indicting the "Mexican" people with the remark, "You are lower than animals and haven't the right to live in organized society—just miserable, lousy, rotten people." In his racist tirade Judge Chargin sanctioned the Jewish genocide program of Nazi Germany and recommended the same for the Mexican people![116] Not as incredible as it may sound, majority society leaders including those in the Jewish community remained intolerably silent.

For the most part, white American citizens have yet to come to the realization that Chicanos are, in actuality, an oppressed non-white American minority at varying levels of interchange as American citizens. Without this acknowledgment anti-Mexicanism and bigotry against brown persons will continue as a negative aspect of the Chicano in southwestern American society. It is unconscionable that the dominant white group can remain insensitive to this issue indefinitely.

---

115. See *Los Angeles Warren Christopher Report*, 1991.

116. *State of California, Court Transcripts, Superior Court of the County of Santa Clara, Juvenile Division*, September 8, 1969.

In all candor, any forthcoming sound resolution lies with educators and politicians. Antagonistic resistance to multiculturalism must cease and be recognized for its long-term past and future potential benefits to American society. It represents the key to improving social interaction between browns and whites. It is not too unlikely a repeat for political power and state separatist aims could emerge in the future should this change fail to materialize.

"False" American idealism with its monocultural and monoracial glorification denies and deprives Chicanos of their fundamental rights of self-determination and freedom as brown Americans. Moreover, in all candor, it is counter-productive and racist to the core. Self-expression is an indispensable human right and need. Anglo, English-speaking exclusivist American supremacism, like other forms of supremacism, is oppressive. And oppression of the spirit is the cruelest poverty of them all. If the psychological apartheid policy of the United States, which is the underlying cause for the evident unchanging underclass position of brown Americans in the new Southwest and California remains unchanged, then we will for some time come to see only *pochos* (pallid faces), and we shall in the end, have defeated our national purpose.

CHAPTER 14

Chicano Nationalism:

A New Birth of Freedom

*T*he sudden-like emergence of a historically unique "Mexican" ethnic social movement gripped the attention of Southwestern and Midwestern Americans where Mexican Americans were clustered in large numbers by the late 1960s. White Americans were bemused by the fact that American "Mexicans" no longer wanted to be American. It was all very strange and perplexing because at the time black Americans were also struggling to gain their American identity hoping to free and liberate themselves from the psychological shackles of delegated second-class citizenship and thinking. Incredible as it may sound, a dominant white American supremacist society had bred an oppressive ambience that begot, of all things, a militant racial reaction and dissidence from stout-colored Americans.

Frankly, the greatest irony was the avante guard of the so-called Chicano Movement. It was composed of many brown Americans who were culturally most Anglo-like. Their English was impeccable and their demeanor and point of reference differed little from socialized white Anglo-Americans. Many of this young generation's cultural point of reference was not hard-core barrio. A relatively significant percentage of them had been reared and nurtured in middle-class white neighborhoods. They were most compatible with the white American mind. Like other Americans they were as critical and dissident as any well-versed white American. They also possessed keen organizational skills and the individuated quest to collectively press the odds to make a difference by changing white American anti-Mexican attitudes.

Since, in fact, so many were not barrio reared or bred many were prompted to seek their identity and their roots. They were motivated to learn about themselves. By this time many had to come to grips with their rather ironic anti-Mexican attitudes, and their shame of being brown-skinned, Spanish-surnamed, and Catholic. They stood apart in white American society. They realized they were resented and despised because they were brown-colored or "Mexican" in southwestern American society. Moreover, they understood through their own personal experience that no matter how hard they tried to be successful in their own right, extraordinary ethnic hurdles had been placed in their way to demotivate and discourage them.

Gradually these young brown-skinned spirits, as if guided by divine direction, spontaneously and uniformly publicly rejected the monocultural and monoracial romanticization of the country's white American legacy. Conversely, white Americans had every intention of keeping it that way—with whites in control. Rash and insensitive resistance fueled greater resolve: what is it "those Mexicans" want? was the common question. Equally foolish and ignorant comments like, "they no longer want to be Americans!" echoed throughout the Southwest and California and elsewhere. Foolish and ignorant because the dissidents they jeered with very few exceptions were born and reared Americans. The obvious difference was that they were brown-skinned Americans with Spanish surnames.

To arrive at a better understanding of the social evolution of American "Mexican" activism and militancy, a number of critical factors demand review. How and why did such intolerable and antagonistic personalities develop? How did all these brown individuals suddenly come together? The answers were not too difficult for students of American ethnic groups. A simple pause helped remind them that colored Americans' quest for freedom and economic opportunities are inevitable in a libertarian and monocultural society like the one in the United States.

Following the Second World War brown Americans were highly motivated to blend into the American society. The new sense of purpose to enjoin with white Americans in pursuit of the American dream of material success was widespread. Mexican Americans left the barrios in appreciable numbers once given the opportunity to live in white American communities. Their children were permitted to attend the same schools alongside white children; an opportunity they had never enjoyed before.[117] But, then, white American society had changed following the war; a conflict that cost millions upon millions of lives.

Nazi and Japanese atrocities against ethnic minorities generated by racial superiority motifs taught white American supremacists a thing or two regarding the form of wicked destruction and suffering vile human ideas take. Moreover, within the last war years, the grave realization that Nazi Germany could still have won the war chilled many bigoted spirits in the United States. The formidable human effort put forth to defeat the Nazi evil had generated a heretofore unmentioned need to work together as a nation to win the war; it required interracial harmony.

War industries generated manpower needs. The challenge to expand war material productivity spurred more equalitarianism for Mexican Americans and Negroes. But it also spawned the growth of new ideas that advanced technological advancements to incredible heights. Americans also became more urbanized so that by the end of the war they were attitudinally more cosmopolitan, equalitarian, and progressive than ever in their history.

Mexican Americans and Chicanos changed, too. An emerging brown American awareness was born and spread across the Southwest. The opportunity to advance materially in American society as an American was something new to the then-Mexican Americans. This was made possible by white American attitudinal changes regarding the colored races. Since white Americans set the standard, and were the socially privileged group, change was possible if they agreed to allow for change to take place. It is hardly arguable that white Americans hold the political policymaking power. Be that as it may, a radically changed Anglo-American social and psychological ambience made it all the more challenging.

In a society wherein accelerated progressive change is most possible, the war and post-war years were most traumatic in that regard. More Americans than ever gave vent to undreamed opportunities to

---

117. In California the *Mendez vs. Westminster* case of 1947 lead to the desegregation of the state's public schools, thereby allowing "Mexican" children to attend school with whites.

pursue their economic dreams to their fullest potential. Maybe now, Mexican Americans and Chicanos believed, they too could earn their own way by merit like other Americans.

The development and intrusion of television and enforced school attendance policies rapidly immersed Mexican Americans in Anglo-American civilization at its best and at its worst. The secular humanist, relativist, and individualist impact of Anglo-American thought among brown Americans was immeasurable; no less so were the basic tenets of American freedom and democracy. But somehow "Mexicans" never really gained the full rights and privileges of American citizenship despite their great sacrifice and contribution during the Second World War and in the Korean War.

Americans gradually recovered from the trauma of the Second World War as they threw themselves into the material prosperity whirlwind generated by an industrialized capitalist war machine. Frankly, physically unscathed from the ravages of war, the United States emerged as the most powerful and prosperous nation on the face of the earth. Gradually, as we noted previously, the vile social faces and vibrations of apartheid reappeared. Social custom was still stronger than constitutional law and the rights of the individual. Clearly that was the case should the object be Negro (black) or Mexican (brown). Nevertheless, it was during this most unique time that Mexican-Americanization social trends peaked.

Roughly speaking, the years between 1945 and 1965 marks the apex in Southwestern American history during which American-born citizens of Mexican descent sought inclusion as full-fledged Americans and earnestly aspired to be as American as time and social circumstance would permit. Many, therefore, cast off their Mexicanness and Chicanoness to accommodate the mandates of the American melting pot, and thereby, to assimilate. Where social custom permitted, many brown Americans moved into housing tracts then being built across the Southwestern United States. The demand for housing by returning servicemen who chose to live in the Southwest and California was met by building immense housing tracts.

The road to social acceptance of Mexican Americans as full-fledged Americans by white Americans was beset with endless social barriers and expected and unexpected qualifications. Are you Spanish? was a common question asked of those who looked "Mexican." An affirmative response suggested to the interrogator that you knew that you knew you were not, but that you would prostitute your integrity and acquiesce for a marginal degree of social acceptance. Whites as the majority pawnbrokers possessed the power to accept or not to accept non-whites as social equals. Attitudes based on race are still similarly governed by that standard. More importantly, racial minorities are still dependent on that standard. Now the reader should bear in mind that in the most too-distant past being white was synonymous with being American. To most whites it still does, although colored and white Americans are a bit wiser now.

Americans are quick to defend and to demand their rights. In fact, given the ambience in which Americans are reared to adulthood, it is beyond debate American culture breeds generally more dissidence than other given national culture. They are doubtless at the top of the humanity heap when it comes to behavioral traits associated with self-centeredness and materialism. They are also more pragmatic, egalitarian, efficient, individualistic, neologistic, and inventive. Most Americans firmly believe in and adhere to the principle of collective power as representative of collective will.

Indeed, most Americans are quick to howl when their individual rights and interests are trespassed, and quick to bemoan tyranny and the loss of other national's human rights. These are basic lessons Americans learn in school, in civic classes, and from their texts. It is part and parcel of being socialized as an American. Chicanos also soon learned the same lessons because they attended the same schools and had the same teachers.

Yet, somehow, the lofty principles of American freedom are still forgotten and ignored by many whites when it comes to black-, brown-, and yellow-skinned Americans. Along the side of goodwill is the great fear of having to share political power and social equality with the black man, the brown man, and yellow man persists. In this connection, American history indicts American society by way of enforced ghettoes for blacks, barrios for Mexicans, reservations for Indians, and Chinatowns for the Chinese. In short, for the implementation of a culture of separation based on race. American racial relations with its own racial minorities is a long endless narrative of sequences of brutality and experiences devoid of compromise. For thinking colored Americans that contradicting legacy is difficult to reconcile, in view of the lessons they learn in school regarding natural rights and the origins of American freedom.

For example, in the recent past, Mexican Americans experiencing melting pot processing somehow found themselves in a quandary. For, they discovered, that regardless how culturally "American" they might be, or even should they be American-born citizens, or that their fathers, sons, and uncles had fought bravely and patriotically in the armed forces like other citizens, they were forevermore accorded a foreign and second-class "Mexican" status. Hyphenated Mexican-American, Hispanic, Latino, Spanish, and Mexican labels were delegated them, never American.

The maturing children of Mexican Americans, who watched the violence of the black civil rights struggle, caught the painful echoes of neo-Chicanos alleging that Chicanos were dying in Vietnam in numbers out of proportion to their population. Somehow they meshed with Cesar Chavez's poor people struggle for justice and economic equity. In this manner a new fight for freedom was born. Suddenly thousands of brown American young people, many of whom were not even Spanish-speaking, clamored: "Ya basta!" "Viva La Raza!" "Yo Soy Chicano!" In retrospect, the mode and the overlooked quest was the group's Americanness. They wanted to be recognized as American, but American in the true sense of the word—free citizens with the same constitutional rights as white Americans. Free to challenge the system, free to demand change. They, unlike their parents, were not content with a powerless hyphenated American status; nor to be like colonized Latinos, Spanish, or Hispanics.

Whether they were American-born did not concern the general public whose sentiments were twisted by decades of anti-Hispano-Mexicanism. A common neo-Chicano, anti-Chicano opinion at the time was: those Mexicans don't want to be American anymore! Although it will probably never be positively determined, perhaps it was this white Anglo racist attitude that encouraged them to find an alternative to the hyphen-less Mexican American term they were initially ascribed. For later they assented to the abbreviated title Chicano used by barrio Chicanos as a casual term of self-identification. They discarded both terms, Mexican and American. In retrospect, that was consistent radical and neologistic American behavior and reasoning.

Thus, they casually connected themselves with barrio Chicanos although most were not barrio reared. Only a few could identify with the culture of the barrio. Many, as we elaborated above, held stronger

Anglo cultural leanings. They were, in effect, neo-Chicano converts with a newfound desire and energy to identify with La Raza of the barrios. In review, it seems that given a racial affinity with barrio people, and because they stemmed from Mexican ancestry, at the time it seemed appropriate for them to use the non-European indigenous term Chicano.

Nevertheless, many Chicano leaders did not particularly approve of their tactics, particularly their self-ascribed leadership roles. Clamoring for attention and notoriety, they often alleged to speak for the barrio communities, which incidentally was resented by the latter who were quick to respond that they had their own grassroots leadership. Curiously, barrio Chicanos considered them *mas agabachados* (more Anglo-like), because their behavior and motivations appeared more like Anglos than like Chicanos or Mexicans.

Conversely, Chicanismo is a time-honored, mentally healthy blend of the two conflicting cultures, that of Mexican and Anglo; in short, it is a historical and sociological harmonious in degree accommodation by Mexican Americans to the predominant secular humanist Anglo-American way of life. But unlike the more culturally harmonized Chicanos, the neo-Chicanos are personalities caught in the throes of an ethnic void because mostly they are in cultural transition. They, consequently, do not affiliate easily due to their imbalance.

As would be expected, to the Mexicans both the Chicanos and the neo-Chicanos are *agringados* (gringo-like). Based on a Mexican point of reference the neo-Chicanos are clearly in degree the more *agringados,* while the barrio Chicanos are the less *agringados.* Both are *agringados,* nevertheless. However, the most irrefutably *agringados* are the brown Anglos; those brown Americans born and reared in a total "gringo" social setting devoid of any contact with barrio Chicanos or Mexicans. The Mexicans, naturally, are persons born and reared in Mexico.

These four major typologies surfaced after a generation of Mexican American exposure to the dominant Anglo American society. It is not a particularly big secret to barrio people whose members readily recognize and acknowledge the differences. The most salient point is recognizing that the vanguard of the Chicano Movement was intensely more neo-Chicano in generation and leadership. Meaning, of course, that it was composed of individuals who had greater affinity to the dominant society than to barrio Chicano society. Most found themselves unable to culturally relate to barrio people. A fact which in great part explains the reason barrio people were unable to totally comprehend the converts' true motivations.

Whatever the case, neo-Chicanos suddenly mobilized and condemned the monocultural educational system. They angrily criticized the process that abused Chicano children, causing them to drop out in such astronomical numbers. Strangely, and perhaps not so, white Anglo educators understood both the neo-Chicanos' motivations and their alternative educational agenda demands. Arguably, it accounted for the uncompromising and formidable Establishment's refusal to change and refusal to yield.

The Establishment had little will or desire to ameliorate via education the social conditions of the dropout rates by permitting multicultural experiences. Collective power-contending persistence effected few changes in the elementary and secondary schools. This attitude in turn fueled the neo-Chicano resolve to demand Chicano Studies departments on the college and university level. The notion of ethnic studies was seen as a necessary progressive step to save La Raza from cultural extinction in concert with all the social ills connected with American Chicano socialization.

Nevertheless, hard-core, vile attitudes, if not programs, did not change slightly. In that connection, it is wondrous and marvelous, indeed, to hear the sounds and intonations of rational acceptance that contribute to an ethnic outsider's feelings of being inside, or at least as a part of the body politic, that in recent memory has so imprudently been denied him. Particularly when that melodic communication is intoned by a once prominent member of the "old white boys club."[118] On February 3, 1992, Arthur Schlesinger, Jr., a Pulitzer-prize-winning historian and former assistant to President John F. Kennedy spoke at the University of Southern California about, of all things, the cult of ethnicity. On the governmental subject of the growing need for multiculturalism in American education he was quite succinct:

> Our public schools, in particular, have been . . . a great agency of assimilation, a great means of transforming newcomers into Americans . . . In a way, the debate about the curriculum is a debate about

---

118. More wondrous, indeed, would be the case if members of the "old white girl's club" would also follow Schlesinger's example.

what it means to be an American. What about multicultural education? When multicultural educations means teaching our kids about
women's history, black history, Latino history, African history, Asian
history—I am all for it . . . And, of course history should be taught
from a variety of perspectives. It is well that our children try to imagine the arrival of Columbus from the viewpoint of those who sent
him. [But] when it calls on education to harden ethnic loyalties and to
promote and perpetuate the separate ethnic and racial communities,
that is a very different matter. Multicultural education in this sense
leads to fragmentation, segregation, ghetto-ism . . . It is not that the
Western cultures are superior to other cultures as much it is, for better or for worse—our culture . . .

At this juncture it is instructive to clear the air a bit. As we previously noted, the culture of separation of ghettos, barrios, Chinatowns,
and tribal American reservations were created and perpetuated by white
members of the American body-politic, with their cruel colonial
supremacist monoculturalist separatist policies. Not by the multicul-
turalists who were its victims.[119] Therefore, Schlesinger's remarks
regarding the supposed "fragmentation, segregation, ghetto-ism" of
multiculturalism are absurdities and figments of his imagination,
because fundamentally, they are not in harmony with historical reality.
Modern multicultural aims are best elucidated in the first part of his
abstracted presentation above.

However, Schlesinger's comments below, if not a cynical misrepre-
sentation, echo the guaranteed natural right tenets of a free people to
retain their cultural identity and their constitutional "right to be"
within the broad and diverse American body politic.

> . . . The aim of education surely should be to strengthen the bonds of
> cohesion, not to weaken them. [Its purpose] should be . . . to show
> minorities have contributed to formation of the common culture and
> the distinctive American identity. Students from a minority back-
> ground should not be herded away among their own, but should be
> taught to become participants and shapers of the common culture.

---

119. Defensive attitude talking by white Americans regarding racial issues invariably aggravates
racism because they refuse to admit they were raised in a racist society, and that the anger
expressed by colored minorities which turns them off is a by-product of an enforced exclusiveness
that bred minority anxiety.

If the student of Chicanismo can fathom this message he will have arrived at the threshold of a more complete and positive understanding of the Chicano experience and its much maligned movement. And, more importantly, on what the movement and the present clamor is really focused.

The most obvious feature is a power contending issue that is analogous to the time of kings and aristocrats, when freedom meant the range of choice for aristocrats only. Freedom in the United States of America has been socially developed to mean freedom and equality for the new self-ascribed white ruling elites. They are in theory and in actuality the new aristocrats. Only they, it has been arrogantly presumed, are privileged to the full range of human experience with all its titles, guaranteed rights, and responsibilities.

Identification as a Chicano is the responsible definition of a brown American's personal humanity and freedom. For any individual the perception of what he is, based on a person's natural right to define and assert his own humanity. That knowledge allows choice and makes responsibility and authority objective realities. Thus, when the law of nature within us, which is our reason, rebels against ethnic tyranny and the oppression or suppression of the group spirit by any form of ethnic cleansing, it is because our humanity and choice are being denied us.

Chicanos, consequently, have the same natural right as anyone else, based on the fundamentals of the natural rights of man on which American constitutional government was established to define, develop, and to live out their personal identity. And, subsequently, the right to live it without being persecuted or oppressed. That condition was irrefutably outlined in the Treaty of Guadalupe Hidalgo of 1848.[120] The treaty incorporated a Hispano-Mexican community into the English-speaking American federation by force of arms and conquest. But, later, resident Mexicans were denied those basic constitutional rights agreed to by treaty by the conquerors.

That might prove difficult for many antagonists to swallow. But as citizens of the United States, Chicanos possess the same rights to criticize, to demand, to expect egalitarian treatment, and to receive due

---

120. *Sublimus Deus,* the so-called doctrine of rationality of Pope Paul III enumerated these same basic rights for the indigenous peoples nearly five hundred years ago in 1537. See Lewis Hanke, *The Spanish Struggle for Justice in the Conquest of America,* (Boston: Little, Brown and Company, 1995) p. 44.

process before the law and respect like all other American citizens. Chicanos are really not demanding more than what is their natural right given their birthright as citizens. The risk of denying them the right to participate in an egalitarian manner, inclusive of the right to prosper materially, portends many potential perilous political and social pitfalls in the future. It is manifest in the message they and other brown Americans have ardently expressed—*"Patria cara, carior libertas."* (My country is dear, but liberty is dearer.)

The civic culture of the United States was born of violence and it absorbs dissidence and dissent after institutional initial resistance. Institutionalization begets assent and is a proven mechanism to claim dissent. A new birth of freedom opened political opportunities for Mexican Americans who sought political office (i.e., as Congressmen). Since the 1980s a growing number of Spanish surnamed politicians have been elected. Many have become insiders. The American institutional system makes them its own. Those brown Americans, whatever their cultural typological reference, who find themselves in the ivory tower subculture or as educators are similarly absorbed. In the following chapters this study will examine in greater depth the brown American labyrinth as Chicanos experience a more subdued anti-Mexican American cultural ambience.

TEACHING CHICANOS HOW TO BEHAVE, THE LITTLE BROWN TOMAS WAY

Mexican Americans were being shaped in the image of white Americans in school and in society generally as we read above, but the anti-Hispano-Mexican legacy was formidable as social custom was set and the culture of separation remained intact. The following excerpt describes the struggle for acceptance in a "false" American way and the rude awakening to the unexpected realities of a space in-between in the ongoing quest for a brown American identity and freedom:

LITTLE BROWN TOMAS BECOMES A MAN

Once upon a time there was a little brown boy named Tomas. He was a shoeshine boy.

"All I want in life," he said, "is to be white, to be equal and to be a man."

Then one day—Hallelujah!—his white masters decreed that he could call himself Caucasian. "Now that you are white," they said, "you must work hard to become equal to us."

Little Brown Tomas nodded. "Yes," he said, "now that I am Caucasian, I must become equal to you so that I, too, can be a man. How do I become equal?"

"The problem," said some Nice White People "is an educational one. You must get an education. Then you will be equal to us."

So some Nice White People gave him an education. It wasn't easy. It took years and years. But at last Little Brown Tomas had an education.

"It's funny," said Tom (for being educated, he had changed his name), "but I still don't feel equal to you."

"The problem," said some Nice White People, "is an economic one. You must have a good job. Then you will equal to us."

So some Nice White People gave Tom a job. It wasn't easy. It took years and years and years. But at least Tom had a good job.

"It's funny," said Tom, "but I still don't feel equal to you."

"The problem," said some Nice White People, "is an environmental one. You must move out of the ghetto into a nice house like ours. Then you will be equal to us."

So some Nice White People got him a house. It wasn't easy. They had to pass laws saying other white people had to sell him a house whether they liked it or not. But at last Tom got a nice house.

"The problem," said some Nice White People "is sociological. You must dress like us, talk like us, and think like us. Then obviously, you will be equal to us."

So some Nice White People taught him to dress and talk and think like whites and they even invited him to cocktail parties.

The hostess would squeeze his hand warmly (though she never kissed him on the cheek.). Then the men would clap him on the back and ask him his opinion (but only about racial matters).

This time, Tom didn't say much at all. He grew a mustache, beard, and changed his name back to Tomas Moreno and shouting "Viva la revolucion" hit the first two Nice White People he saw over the head.

They were of course, deeply hurt. "After all we've done for you," they said.

"Don't you realize you're throwing away everything we struggled together for? Now you'll never feel equal to us."

"It's funny," said Tom smiling, "but at last I feel like a Man."

Aware of his culturally marginal status groomed by following the recommendations of some Nice White People, Tomas enrolled in Chicano Studies to reclaim his identity and to bond with other Chicanos.

Some Nice Brown Professors taught him about Marx, Fanon, and post-colonialism,

He also learned about oppression, resistance, Freire, Che Guevara, and revolution,

Some Nice Brown Professors blasted the cultural nationalist Chicano Movement despite the many social gains as separatist, sexist, and homophobic.

Also, that the Catholic Church was the oppressive enemy, and religious writing was done by men to control women,

Tomas was turned off reading about non-Chicano revolutionaries,

And, the antagonism for the religious values of La Raza,

Tomas reflected, "They are just like the *gabachos,* their goal is the same. To reshape my mind by shredding my Chicano image."

Then, Tomas, smirked and shook his head, "I thought I was *agabachado,* but these Nice Brown College People *son los mas agabachados.*"

Tomas dropped out of college and Chicano Studies and went back to the so-called ghetto (the barrio) to work with less-educated *locos,* the *batos locos.*

"Boy, what a mess," Tom thought, "It is hard to be a brown Man!!"

CHAPTER 15

Freedom Maligned:

The Pathways of "False" Americanism

*T*he new birth of freedom was in part successfully achieved by Chicano militants. Chicano Studies programs incorporated in university and college academic programs are living proof of its success. As an academic discipline it was novel for both Chicanos and white Americans who did not particularly appreciate Chicano Studies as an academic discipline. They were still caught in the pathways of "false" Americanism better known as the melting pot. Needless to say, republican Protestantism, which is synonymous for "False" Americanism, had pervaded brown American thought and behavior in many cases beyond redemption to the regret of many Chicanos because they are lost as leaders to the Mexican American community. And, lamentably, with the worst possible scenario of they becoming adversaries of communal Chicano reform as *vendidos.*

The first decade of the Chicano Movement between 1968 and 1978 illustrated that psychological division quite well. A diversity of cultural typological dimensions was most self-evident as previously noted in Chapter 13. University and college Chicano Studies departments were a clinical window case study. Nevertheless, regardless of cultural or political differences, they overcame potential and psychological disharmony to collectively challenge the country's racist anti-Hispano-Mexican legacy. Frankly, much to their credit and in spite of the cultural diversity and extent of distinctive Mexican and Chicano borders and the "false" American de-socialization experience of the previous decade that they, except for a very small minority, came together in collective protest was remarkable.

What is of greater significant interest, however, is the fact that the initial intellectual query for brown liberation originated with Mexican-born individuals and one very brilliant Native American. Professor Jack D. Forbes was the Native American whose pre-Chicano Movement pro-indigenous and Mexican American ideas influenced the emergence of the original Mexica Movement, which cultivated indigenous-ism, and stirred the academic challenges and innovations of Professor Octavio Romano with his publications of Quinto Sol, and the poetry of Alurista, both Mexico-born men. Their actions then saw Mexico-born professor, Juan Gomez-Quinones add to seminal Chicano scholarship with the Aztlan journal for Chicano authors.

Then, unexpectedly anti-Chicano Movement rhetoric originated with Mexican born and reared women or non-Chicano Latinas. The cause for these oppositional ideologies was their cultural perspective. Clearly, the Mexican males like Romano and Alurista were not culturally alienated. They obviously possessed little if any minority anguish which would have derailed any positive constructive developments. They were clear-minded and realistic regarding the greater picture. Indeed they had nothing to prove to the *gabacho* Establishment. Conversely, the Mexican women were not in concert with Mexican culture although they were Mexican nationals then resident in the United States. Their oppositional role influenced some Chicanos but mostly the neo-Chicanos who were in fact not part of, or were culturally alienated from their Chicano culture.

For whatever personal purpose or whatever motivated them, Mexicans, socialists, communists, anarchists, feminists, Chicanos, atheists, Protestants, and humanists joined the university and college Mexican American Movement. It was not a barrio community-led movement. It is superfluous to assume women, homosexuals, and lesbians also participated. The cultural nationalist political center mandated rigid conformity and loyalty. It was not separatist, it was exposing the American culture of separation which was, frankly, the common denominators that energize the participants and was their ultimate frustration with the anti-Mexican legacy, racism of the academy and society. And, the acknowledged reality that most were marginalized Americans treated like second-class citizens, separate and unequal.

That the group was a politically powerless and despised racial lower-class community was most resented. They initiated a new challenge for American society, i.e., public demonstrations. The meek, docile, humble Mexican psychology was absent because these were Mexican American products of American schools. "Seeing Mexican demonstrations against racism and injustice on college and high school campuses and in city streets and yelling Viva La Raza," was novel for Mexican Americans and white Americans. Surely, such American-like political behavior had never been seen among Chicanos. Plainly, the activists were not marginalized *pachucos* and this was not the 1940s, and the demonstrators were not Mexicans.

GENDER-CENTRIC VOICES NOT OF OR FOR LA RAZA

It is noteworthy that the National Organization of Women (N.O.W.) was similarly active during this decade. Black civil rights demonstrations and the Vietnam War stirred many Americans to serious introspection. The woman's group's quest to recruit and attract new adherents demanded that the movement not lose momentum as a result of divided ideological differences. To secure its philosophical focus and momentum they required that the many socialists and lesbians among their ranks take a back seat so as not to discourage potential new members. The common feeling among many Americans was that N.O.W. was born of socialist ideology and that most of its membership was lesbians.[121] The truth is, many were. Nevertheless, their strategy was effective as ideological division did not incur serious divisions to defuse the thrust of the movement. Minority-colored women shunned the movement due to the racist mode then current in American society. Social contact between whites and minority groups was peripheral. They correctly perceived it as a middle-class white woman's movement. Nevertheless, some brown socialists and culturally marginalized women naturally were influenced by their radical ideas as we will illustrate in this chapter.

The Plan de Aztlan which set the format for Chicano liberation and Chicano Studies had a singular purpose, too—the liberation from "false" Americanism and the racist and unjust oppression of all Mexican Americans. It did not categorize, i.e., did not single out women,

---

121. *The Los Angeles Times,* September 5, 1971. N.O.W. "assailed the actions of groups and organizations, including the socialists, seeking to drive a wedge into the woman's Movement."

homosexuals, or lesbians. It was a communal confrontation. The movement followers mobilized to reconfigure *gabacho* stereotypical thinking regarding the social status of brown-skinned, Spanish-surnamed, Spanish-speaking, Catholic Chicanos. As noted above, neo-Chicanos glorified Mexican culture to establish an ethnic political message and an ethnic bond; to demonstrate that they were proud of being of Mexican descent.

Like the N.O.W. group the neo-Chicano movement leadership saw little political gain in subjecting its movement to divisive categories either by referencing socialists or women although N.O.W., for example, did support the lesbian social agenda. Nevertheless, for a Spanish-surnamed woman like Mary Pardo to label the Plan de Aztlan a "man-ifesto" and for Mexican American women in their gender-centric neo-Chicana movement that emerged in the early 1980s, to discredit the Chicano Plan for resistance as sexist because it lacked a "feminist" vision to Chicanos is the height of unmitigated gall. Frankly, it is a shame that the split they have created has been so acrimonious. But rancor it is because of its insensitive, arrogant, and self-serving clamor. Plainly, their political posture is devoid of collective Chicano *amor propio*. The sexist allegation disregards the vile social conditions at the time of the birth of the Chicano Movement. White American anti-Mexicanism and racism was virulent. That social climate was no academic or intellectual game, as it was pernicious, cruel, and unforgiving beyond decent human understanding, and it still is.

Racist white moms nurtured hatred in their children of Chicanos including Chicano mothers, wives, and sisters. The object of their venom was racial, not gender-centric. That racial hatred still stings and is unchanged given the out-of-proportion school Chicano dropout figures. And because of that racial divide Chicanos continue to fill the jails and prisons. Many are marginalized and caught in an emotional limbo of psychological confusion which retards their unity, material progress, and basic freedoms as Chicanos. Worse yet, most still don't feel equal. Therefore, to read the scurrilous commentaries of Chicano culture and the cultural nationalist movement as separatist by self-ascribed neo-Chicanos justifies resentment against them because the struggle is far from over. Even if the critics are insensitive Chicano pretenders.

Whatever, they were at odds with Chicanismo and Chicano self-determination, they were unable to comprehend or to relate to the political intent and implications of flaunting Mexicanism in Anglo-American society. Their objection was and is irrefutably anti-Mexican which explains their defensiveness. However, it should be made clear that if they were isolated and reared beyond the borders of the Chicano barrio experience of itself did not automatically make them *vendidas* or sellouts. No! But the self-ascribed false claim to being Chicana to gain *gabacho* commendation in order to discredit and mock La Raza as Chicana pretenders or *falsas* does earn them that disreputable label. Psychologically, as one Chicana asserted, "they are not of our people."

Moreover, the Chicano definition of the much misunderstood *vendida* label is not based on deviation from motherhood or nurturer, religion or gender role-playing either. Without being redundant it should be recognized that many critical brown women were or are either brown Anglos, Mexicans, Protestants, lesbians, and socialists. They were not cultural Chicanas and thereby unable to relate to the Chicano cultural experience. As converts to a neo-Chicana idea, they are political Chicanas. Frankly, in many cases given their distinctive cultural and ideological background it is questionable whether they are committed wannabe Chicanas to begin with. However, given their resistance and criticism to cultural neo-Chicanismo suggests many are not really ideological converts either.

In addition, they stereotype barrio and committed Chicanas with the label "loyalists" with the inference the latter are incapable of making correct choices and reasoning for themselves. In short, their quest appears to be driven by being label-connected with the Chicano community as peripheral converts for validation or for some attention acquiring purpose. And, since they propose to reconfigure Chicano culture, at least in their writings and in their classrooms, opportunistically as self-ascribed leaders and intellectuals with the Chicana label, it is the *gabacho's* approbation they aspire. This psychological analysis holds true for Aspirant and brown Anglo males as well.

"NOT LIKE THE GABACHAS," BUT
GENDER-CENTRIC ANYWAY

Enmity toward glorified Mexicanism and Catholicism expressed during the self-ascribed Chicana Conference held in Houston, Texas, in 1971 is singular because considerable reference is made of that event in brown feminists' writings today. The conference was hosted by the

Young Woman's Christian Association with a tailored anti-Catholic agenda. Some of the participants came to the early conclusion that the hosts were resolved on encouraging a gender chasm in the Chicano Movement which pitted brown women against brown men. Be that as it may, the following Conference anti-Catholic and anti-Mexican resolutions were self-evident: "Free legal abortions . . . liberate your mind and your body will follow . . . we should destroy the myth that religion and culture control our lives . . . we, *mujeres* . . . recognize that the Catholic Church as an oppressive institution and do thereby resolve to break away and not go to it to bless our unions . . . oppose any institutionalized religion." And, echoing verbatim the N.O.W. platform on the bible religion ". . . religious writings was done by men and interpreted by men!" Thus, denials how these alleged Chicanas were not influenced by N.O.W and socialism are irrefutably false.

One should not look beyond the fact that college and university students and non-Catholic brown women tend to be more liberal regarding abortion and sexual practices than the average citizen. Catholic Chicanas don't need pro-choice laws regarding abortion and pre-marital sex. Like all Catholics the choice on abortion or sexual license is a matter of conscience. Non-Catholic atheists and socialists adhere to their subjective volition. Pro-choice in their case is a legal secular issue.

Abortion was legalized in 1967 in California and in Colorado. In 1973 the *Roe vs. Wade* legislation made the process legal nationally. From its very inception abortion was promoted by liberal middle-class white women. Up to that time it was illegal. Indeed, around the time of the women's liberation movement between 1966 and 1967 a survey of 5,300 Mexican couples was compiled by Maria Leñero. *Hacia donde va la mujer mexicana?,* included questions on abortion. A comparable review is particularly revealing.

Leñero found that forty percent of married Mexicans surveyed would favor abortion if the mother's life was in danger and twenty-five percent in the event of abnormalities. This position was taken despite the fact most respondents were Catholic. The same study illustrated they were aware of all the possible birth control methods. Seventy-five percent of the woman and seventy-four percent of the men were aware of the oral pill. As for the concocted notion by white American feminists that Mexican "macho" men rejected the use of condoms because it diminished pleasure or for religious scruples the responses in

Leñero's study do not support that off-the-cuff notion. Nine percent of female respondents and thirteen percent of the male respondents agreed it was ineffective. As for religious scruples, less than one percent of the women and nine percent of the male respondents claimed that was the reason they abandoned birth control methods.

In a comparable and contemporary study of Mexican American students in Los Angeles County, California, during the years 1973–1976 The Orozco Report profiling Mexican American College and University students revealed that they were quite conservative regarding abortion. Eighty-one percent claimed to be Catholic. Regarding abortion the respondents were more conservative than the Mexicans. Eighteen percent when the mother's life is in danger. Thirteen-and-a-half percent when abnormalities are possible. Thus, it appears much of what was presumed to have been negative by neo-Chicanas and other brown American critics was not affirmed by these surveys. Even an American Catholic Survey for the same period illustrated more liberal attitudes as 80% of the respondents were pro-abortion.

"OUR CULTURE HELL" GLORFIED
MEXICANISM MALIGNED

While the Houston Conference was a serious attack on the Chicano Movement, another example of an anti-Mexicanism essay widely circulated was by Guadalupe Valdes Fallis, a Spanish-surnamed female writer of unknown ethnic background. Valdes Fallis authored a blatant anti-Mexican essay in the 1974 journal "Women, a Journal of Liberation." It was uncertain whether she was Mexican-reared, a brown Anglo, a socialist, or a neo-Chicana. Valdes Fallis outlined and accented almost verbatim the radical philosophy of the then-emerging white woman's liberation movement. Valdes Fallis was college educated. She received her doctorate in education and Languages in 1972. That was in total contrast to most Chicanos. In the early 1970s most Chicanos were still insulated in barrio life locked in by the American Culture of Separation. A very small number had matriculated into college as the high school dropout rates were high.

Frankly, throughout the Southwest and California many Mexican Americans were farm laborers, migrant workers, and working class. In other words they worked with their hands and backs. Also, a large majority was poor or near the poverty line. But they were American-schooled being American citizens. Therefore, when Guadalupe Valdes Fallis lashed out like an elitist against the glorification of Mexican culture and tradition in the Movement it was one of the first most Anglo-American-like anti-Mexican harsh criticisms at the time. The fact it was printed in *Women: A Journal of Liberation* was self-evident the author sang in white American intonations.

Fallis's condemnations echoed the stereotypical works of Mexican Americans by Celia Heller Tuck, William Madsen, Robert Hayden, Norman D. Humphrey, and others condemned by the anthropologist Octavio Romano and early Chicano Movement scholars.[122] Without reference to race, class, urban, or rural cultures Ms. Fallis wrote ". . . The Mexican woman is born to suffer." "The male of the Spanish tradition wants yet fears sexuality in 'his' woman." Now, it should be noted that by the 1970s Mexican American women were not quite traditional, hardly like Mexican women. They represented the first Mexican American generation massively educated and socialized on American democracy in the public schools following World War II.

Moreover, as we noted in Chapter 13, although they were bilingual and bicultural, most Mexican Americans were leaning toward English language usage and assimilation into American life. Indeed, although not completely culturally Anglo American, they most certainly were not Mexican. Still, they were more conservative than most white Americans. As a minority ethnic group Mexican Americans were comparable to other working-class Americans by the 1970s. And, a growing number were exogamous.

Nevertheless, Valdes Fallis completely dismissed the dehumanizing and disheartening causes of unemployment, poverty, and racism in concert with the anti-Hispano Mexican legacy of the Southwest and California. Given that she was also oblivious to the major causes that sanctioned the Chicano Movement suggests she was not culturally sensitive. In step with other feminists, whether Mexican born and reared, Aspirants or socialists, she failed to grasp the cultural distinction between Mexicans and Chicanos. To Chicanas Valdes Fallis paternalistically wrote: "She needs to understand who the main oppressors in the life of her sisters have been . . ." "The traditions which historically

---

122. Miguel Montiel, "The Social Science Myth of the Mexican American Family," *El Grito, A Journal of Contemporary Mexican American Thought,* Vol. II, No. 1 (Fall, 1968), p. 63.

What are your personal feelings regarding the practice of abortion?

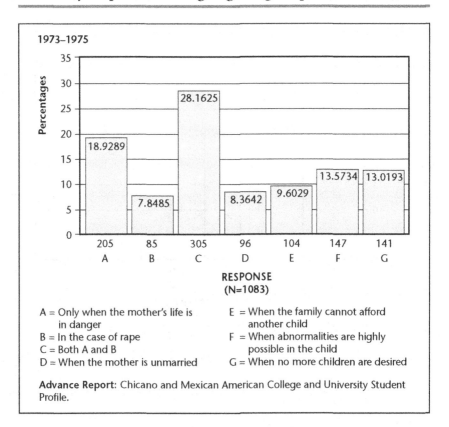

1973–1975

A = Only when the mother's life is in danger
B = In the case of rape
C = Both A and B
D = When the mother is unmarried

E = When the family cannot afford another child
F = When abnormalities are highly possible in the child
G = When no more children are desired

Advance Report: Chicano and Mexican American College and University Student Profile.

have been used to lock Chicana women in a subordinate role are still being glorified."

Clearly, during the early years of the Chicano Movement the radical feminist movement and the ivory tower impacted neo-Chicana thought. Since no survey or studies were taken of Chicano Movement participant responses regarding the conference in Houston or writers like Fallis, they were generally regarded as *vendidas.* It meant they were doing the white man's work as Chicanas *falsas.* Those individuals whether male or female who took the *gabacho* side were highly resented. Which, in retrospect, the then defensive and most definitively appropriate statement proclaimed by the Chicana pretenders or *falsas* was, "Our culture, hell!" For, yes, it was not their culture. They were of the false opinion they were Chicanos because they were of Mexican descent.

Did males receive special treatment in your family?

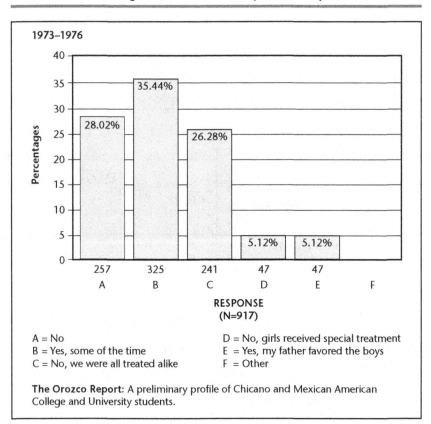

1973–1976

A = No
B = Yes, some of the time
C = No, we were all treated alike

D = No, girls received special treatment
E = Yes, my father favored the boys
F = Other

The Orozco Report: A preliminary profile of Chicano and Mexican American College and University students.

Furthermore, liberal whites, unless they were communists or pros-elytizing Protestants, never supported the Chicano Movement. In fact, sectarian Protestant universities were unwilling to establish studies pro-grams for their Mexican American students because its cultural foun-dations were basically Catholic. Consequently, the support now given the neo-Chicana movement by the ivory tower, white feminist radicals, and liberals is novel. The question might be asked: Is it because the self-ascribed neo-Chicanas are more culturally and philosophically com-patible with whites by way of their insensitive and antagonism toward Chicanismo, Mexicanism, and Catholicism? If so, then the cultural typologies discussed in this study make it self-evident brown people are not homogeneous.

GAY LIFE: A CHICANO PERSPECTIVE

Brown feminists have modeled the white woman's liberation movement and socialism in many ways, including their novel interest in homosexuality. In their quest to appear progressive, Aspirants write that Chicano culture and the Movement were homophobic and patriarchal. Yet, homosexuality was not a topic of empathy during black civil rights or during the Chicano Movement. Racism was the major gnawing issue for the colored minorities, white liberals, and white university women. In fact, white university women consorted publicly with black men for the first time in American history to express their disgust for white American racism. In fact, not even on university campuses were gay empathies an issue. The Aspirants and particularly brown women like most critics and proponents of homosexual political agendas often look beyond the fact that in states like California sodomy was a crime and cohabitation without a marriage license was highly frowned upon. Sodomy laws were repealed during the height of black civil rights and the Chicano Movement in 1976 in California. Nevertheless, homosexuality was not a problem among barrio Chicanos. But it was in the civic culture of the country due to historical and legal reasons.

In fact, homophobic roots in American society are deep-rooted. During the colonial period when homosexuality was a capital offense, Thomas Jefferson who wrote the American Declaration of Independence, advanced the idea that homosexuals should be castrated.[123] A 2007 PEW Research Center Global Project Attitudes Study revealed that homophobia is a less evident negative sentiment in Catholic countries. Of relevant interest to our study in the same report is that homophobia is a greater social disease in the United States than in Mexico. The rejection of homosexuality in the United States and in Mexico is forty-one percent and thirty-one percent, respectively. Sixty-one percent accept homosexuality in Mexico compared to forty-nine percent in the United States.[124]

In the United States adult Chicanos and even the *batos locos* in the barrios don't even blink at gay behavior. So much for the negative stereotype of homophobic macho Mexican and Chicano culture. A

---

123. Louis Crompton, "Homosexuals and the Death Penalty in Colonial America," *Journal of Homosexuality*, Vol. 1, (3), 1976, p. 286.

124. "Pew Global Attitudes Survey: Views of Religion and Morality," Pew Research Center, Washington, D.C. Oct. 4, 2007.

Catholic homosexual has no issue so long as he does not succumb to his sexual inclinations as is the case with heterosexual persons. Restraint and repression of irresponsible sexual practices is the norm. To Catholics it is a matter of conscience.

The status of homosexuality is an on-going civil or political issue in the secular United States, not a theological one. It is not a major Chicano issue although brown feminists have forcefully sought to make it one in their theoretical disquisitions.[125] Discrimination for the love of God or in "God's eyes" of unacceptable carnal practices like active homosexuality is a civil offense in a secular society. It is without question an important difference given the decree of social tolerance in the one versus the other. The clash is related to what is moral behavior in the religious circles versus the secular life. Racism is a sin in dogmatic Christian religion but an infringement of a person's civil rights in the City of Man. In their consistency many trendy neo-Chicanas again enjoined a *gabacho* popular secular political topic by interjecting the homophobic issue as a major Chicano liberation factor. And, of course, by the inference that Chicano culture is homophobic however devoid of any scientific survey to support the allegation.

---

125. Aida Hurtado, "*Sitios y Lenguas:* Chicanas theorize feminisms," *Hypatia,* Vol. 13(2) Spring, 1998, pp. 134–161.

CHAPTER 16

Anything but Chicano Thought

*F*rom the very inception of the Chicano Movement the socialists were at odds with Chicano cultural communalism. Their quest was for a socialist communalism that was more universal, a central concept evident in brown feminists' efforts to redefine Chicanismo. Unlike N.O.W. proponents, who requested socialists not divide the woman movement's unity although much of their philosophy was filtered with Marxist thought, the Chicano Movement leadership neglected to require a similar policy regarding socialism. In actuality it was due to the small number of brown professors in the ivory tower and because some socialists were active leaders in the Movement from the start. Thus, the current ideological rift that is most evident in Chicano Studies programs had its origin from the onset with non-Chicano political issues such as socialism and radical brown feminism.

The ideological contest has deep roots. Efforts by socialist groups to recruit Chicano adherents have been many. The pamphlet "Chicano Liberation and Socialism" by Miguel Pendas was viewed as too radical by Chicano activists in the 1970s. Moreover, it was generally dismissed by most participants because it did not relate to immediate Chicano life issues and their quest for ethnic liberation and civil reform. Socialism was more attractive to Aspirant neo-Chicano reformers for whom it served as a middle comfort zone between Chicanismo and that of becoming a full-fledged *gabacho*. The new *nepantla* or *mestiza* notion ideally serves as that redefined "Chicana" zone for female Aspirants or

Chicana pretenders. The other earlier oppositional preference was to be humanistic without appearing neutral than to be cultural nationalist in which exclusivity was expected. The fervent wannabe indigenous types rejected the Hispanic trappings of Chicanismo often inclusive of the Catholic religion.

Given the vast number of marginal Chicano personalities that were and are susceptible to cure-all ideologies and religions is not a novel expectation. Because of that psychological diversity, classroom ideas and particularly socialism attracts some as a definitive course of action to reform a society that oppresses them and which they despise. Paulo Freire's soft socialism with its more progressive educational pedagogies is popular among marginalized personalities. To some neo-Chicanos Freire offers an effective ideal counter or auxiliary methodology to the secular humanist American public schools educational philosophy framed by John Dewey. The disenchanted marginal personality seeks ready-made systems as templates by which it hopes to reconfigure the educational philosophy of America's public school system. Motivated and energized by a helplessness that is often characteristic of a marginal personality nurtured by years of frustration, social activism drives them. The fall of the Iron Curtain mercifully significantly defused a great deal of socialist fervor and idealistic militancy.

There was also the liberation theology-like spiritual activism conjured up by Gloria Anzaldua with its camouflaged socialist trappings in the 1980s which attracted some Aspirants and wannabe Chicanas. One must bear in mind that social activism is the dissidents' diet and there were more than enough social issues to stimulate their socialist reformist cortical impulses and appetites during the hectic and disordered decade of the 1970s and early 1980s. Surely, while Chicana pretenders alleged that it was done for Chicanismo, that was and is not always necessarily the case because it is an alienating process that further distanced them from the very community they allegedly were struggling to liberate. Certainly actions speak louder than words.

Anzaldua, whose book *Borderlands/La Frontera; The New Mestiza,* endeared her to *gabachas* and many marginalized brown women, admitted that she deliberately broke away from the Chicano community she did not particularly appreciate when she entered college. Upon her return to a Chicano ambience, her personal quest was to reconfigure the Chicano sense of community based on her expanded perspectives. In light of these actions the question then emerges: Was her redefining ends elitist or perhaps just a case of a self-serving marginal personality bent on uplifting her perception of Chicanos from what she determined to be their cultural hang-ups?

Now, little basis for debate exists that Mexican American like Afro-American defiance is nurtured by ethnic oppression in the United States beginning in our public schools. Marginal personalities have the right to their anger and frustration. And, they also possess the right to collectively seek solutions to their oppression like Anzaldua and others have attempted. However, it does not entitle any of them to return from college "white-washed" or ideologically converted and to then, like elitists, attempt to reconfigure Mexican American society. Particularly, if they have ventured beyond its cultural borders and values systems they never related to in the first place. Anzaldua's feminism brought sexuality to the center more forcefully and it was to be connected to lesbianism. And, she has many disciples. As many thinking barrio Chicanos have wondered and asked, what is their problem?

NON CHICANO COMMUNALISM: "CITIZENS OF THE UNIVERSE"

In retrospect, it was interesting the varied cultural typologies and ideologies that emerged at the height of the Chicano Movement. The so-called left wingers were especially active. Whether they were driven by a communist or socialist objective like Rodolfo Acuna, Bert Corona, Tomas Almaguer, Olga Talamante, Natividad Lopez, Manuel de Ortega, Damian Garcia, Rosalio Munoz, and many closet socialists, although not united they influenced those who would be shaped by their socialist activism and visionary regeneration or reconfiguration of the social status quo.[126] Surely, it is beyond debate that socialists were

---

126. Damian Garcia of San Bernardino, California, radicalized by the racist society in which he was reared, joined the Revolutionary Communist Party. He and a companion, on March 20, 1980, raised the communist red flag of revolution on the Alamo shrine in Texas, the U.S. symbol of U.S. domination over Mexico and a symbol of hatred of Mexican Americans. He was murdered a month later in Los Angeles' Pico Gardens housing project preparing for revolutionary actions on May 1. See photo of his memorable retaking of the Alamo in *Orozco, Republican Protestant in Aztlan*, op. cit., p. 229.

Rudy Acuna was Plenary Speaker at the Scholars West Coast Socialist Conference on April 16–17, 1993, at UCLA in which he stated that he was more to the left of the socialists present at the conference.

Olga Talamante was arrested in Argentina for alleged anti-government socialist activities.

active in the struggle against racism and anti-Mexicanism but their objectives were congruent with international third world class issues. Class infrastructures rooted in economic imbalances and class exploitation were more central to their sensitivities than the immediate racial or cultural concerns of Chicano activists.

Ethnicity is not of grave concern to a socialist except as an instrument by which to gain adherents and collectivize to make a political statement. Race and culture are dismissed as major causative factors. Socialists focus more on class struggle between the working class and the status quo. In their view, that struggle sanctions radicalism and activism. Professor Acuña concurred in his popular book, *Occupied America,* that socialist communalism fragmented movement goals but that it brought in the class struggle issue more openly. In this perspective one can presume race was related to class as a major issue. Since 1848 Mexicans have been considered lower class culturally and racially by white Americans because they are colored skinned and presumed to be mixed with Native Americans.

Two types of Chicanos emerged during the movement: first, the less numerous Chicanos who were born and reared in the barrios, and second, those non-barrio Chicanos who were committed to self-determination, freedom from oppression, and Chicano Studies. The second were actually political converts to a cause. They were the neo-Chicanos. Nevertheless, for a Chicano Studies scholar the political and cultural chasm is self-evident when a brown author chides Chicano culture and focuses instead on post-colonial feminism, transnationalism issues, and lesbian sub-culture. The focus is self-evident. Chicano culture is an established culture. A barrio Chicana is culturally aware of what comes first. It is not just a label of a person being of Mexican descent born in the United States. With feminism, in effect, the resolve is to be an individual *ala a gabacha* (me, I, ego) rather than a communal person (us, we) in the struggle for social liberation, justice, and equality.

Non-barrio brown feminists were forced to resolve the simple equation. Thus, two theoretical alternatives were created by these feminists. One, they had to redefine Chicanismo, or promote the anti-colonial internationalism without borders as in socialism, or the new "space between" promoted by the likes of Anzaldua and non-Chicano intellectuals. Since many brown women authors were isolated from barrio or Mexican life their intellectual disquisitions were basically analogous to those of a socialist's grand "classroom noble idealism." Socialist reform? In historical retrospect, it was a failed dream for millions elsewhere, long before they imagined they could alter hundreds of years of universal human social patterns, values, mores, and misogyny with one crushing titanic blow.

Lacking a communal unity with La Raza many brown feminists parroted their *gabacha* and *gabacho* professors. They read the inspired words of the marginalized black intellectuals like Frantz Fanon and others. Socialist ideas persisted as ideal anti-capitalist counters among some neo-Chicanas. Indeed, some even visited the Soviet Union and Cuba, who knows for whatever reason. In fact, one of the ivory tower's brown intellectual favorites ascribed "che" to her middle name to honor the brutal revolutionary Che Guevara who murdered entire Cuban families. Progressively, neo-Chicanas became disciples of non-Chicano theorists to formulate templates to further liberate themselves and their disciples from colonized Anglo-Americanism or Chicanismo, or both. Yet, in their liberation quest they embrace and perpetuate the colonizing Chicano terms Latino and *mestizo* as if they were positive labels. Liberal ivory tower icons like Fanon, Michel Foucault, Chandra Mohanty, Homi Bhabha, and Gayatri Spivak joined the likes of Karl Marx for their preferred ideological templates.

But the actual colonialism neo-Chicanas assail escapes them because they are not in harmony with the historical reality according to the self-proclaimed post-Marxist Jose Rebasa. Rebasa, however critical of Spanish colonialism, skirts the true origins that drive post-colonialism. In his book, *Writing Violence on the Northern Frontier,* Rebasa is fully aware that the post-colonialism condemned by Fanon, Mohanty, Foucault, and others is not inclusive of the Spanish so-called "shared" colonialism "of three centuries earlier," but rather of Asian and African histories over a century ago in the late 1880s. Yet, anti-Hispanic minds like Rebasa persist in the idea that the conquest of the Aztecs and the three hundred years of Spanish colonialism does apply. These views, upon closer analysis, are inaccurate delusions of marginal minds not versed in objective history. Frankly, the point was made by one famous ancient philosopher who eternalized the saying that "the enemy of truth is the unversed mind."

The brown non-Chicano agenda is self-evident in their essays that promote ideology, not scholarship. Their intention is to indoctrinate, not to inform. Rather than to concentrate on teaching Chicano students about who they are, they prefer to teach Chicanos who and what they should be in a global, international, or universal context. They guide them toward socialism or to the so-called new *nepantla* of the self-ascribed "citizen of the universe" Gloria Anzaldua who noted she transported herself beyond Chicano borders, at least in her mind. And, strangely since one of the major goals of the Chicano Movement sought to democratize and reconfigure *gabacho* society, the socialists and many feminists instead seek to individuate and reconfigure cultural Chicanos because they cannot relate to a culture based on a Catholic communalism they resent. It then becomes obvious that their aim is to further de-socialize the marginal Chicanos from their Hispano-Mexican roots.

THE EMPOWERMENT OF ANTI-CLERICAL PATHWAYS

In attacking the secular *gabacho* Establishment of which they are often a definite part and which is the cause of many social ills among Chicanos, alleged neo-Chicanas like the N.O.W. leadership drifted into the periphery of theology. And, in so doing like white radical feminists they dismissed the fact that theology is neither democratic nor secular. The first mandates reason over matter. In the second, the secular mind succumbs to human instinct and desire. The first is God-centered communalism while the latter is individualistic and man-centered. The ideological clash discussed above crystallized among brown women. Neo-Chicanas learned from the likes of N.O.W. Christian religion and patriarchy could be criticized and attacked without serious recrimination.

They emphasized the notion that since men wrote the Bible, this justified the abandonment of religion. Men made all the rules to control and subordinate women, and it was not inspired or ordained by God. Moreover God was genderless, God was an IT, not a He the Father. Coincidentally, the snowballing anti-dogmatic religion drive followed the historical sequential pathways of the Freemasonic founding fathers of the United States. Agnosticism and Deism were popular then. Most of the founding fathers were Deists. Their God was the God of Reason and the God of the ancient Greek philosophers. Furthermore, hippies were also very active during the Civil Rights decade and their clamor was ironically similar. To the hippies, God was dead.

Actually, these neo-Chicanas flushed with feminist empowerment ideals which were filtered with socialist and "false" American repugnance for dogmatic religion stumbled into the not so novel ancient clash between theology and science. Moreover, like true socialists and secular humanists, they condemn the Catholic religion for its dogmatic conventional doctrine against abortion, homosexuality, and birth control. The pro-abortion issue was one of the most interesting because in actuality most women failed to take into account that it sanctions irresponsible male behavior and the abuse of women. Abortionists make money and most of them just happen to be men, too. These brown women, nevertheless, denounced and resented dogmatic religion which is the cultural bond of Mexicanism and Chicanismo. The neo-Chicanas also assailed the institution of the Chicano family as a tender trap of *madrecita* because they sacrifice themselves for the comfort of others. They perceived the family as patriarchal and traditional. In this manner, the neo-Chicanas were echoing the credos of most secular and Protestant white Americans both of whom are anti-traditional and anti-dogmatic religion.

True to American secular humanism, as we observed above, in their quest for political empowerment as women these feminists have learned to attack dogmatic religion in a manner reminiscent of the founding fathers of the United States who unabashedly mocked Christian religion for the same reason. Many of the founding fathers were Freemasons and anti-Christian. They lauded the mocked resurrection scene of Jesus Christ in an oil painting in which the image of George Washington had replaced the risen Christ.[127] Alma Lopez, a lesbian artist, in similar secular mocking fashion transformed the Virgin de Guadalupe, a Mexican and Chicano Catholic icon, irrevently by transforming her image into a secular liberated nearly naked attractive *nalgona* with a naked angel at her feet.[128] Perhaps as secular art it was meant to depict more appropriately a *Virgen de las jotas*? But as intended the artist's depiction offended non-college Mexican Americans and conservative Catholics when it was displayed publicly in art shows. Lopez expressed disappointment that the Pope had not condemned it so she could have

---

127. Alma Lopez's sexual provocative "art" suggests a very American secular mind-set for it is comparable with the anti-Christian Freemasonic portrait of George Washington. See E.C. Orozco, *Republican Protestantism in Aztlan*, Regina Books, 2010, p. 73.

128. Church Councils from the second century affirmed the Blessed Virgin Mary as *theotokos* (god-bearer or the mother of God) as opposed to *cristotokos* (the mother of Christ). She is also known as the "spouse of the Holy Spirit." Pope John Paul II officially validated the apparition of Santa Maria de Guadalupe in Mexico He visited the shrine twice.

sold more copies of her lesbian art creation which she created with obvious intent to upset brown Catholics although she claimed that was not her intention.

Thus, disoriented, alienated, confused, and hostile brown personalities who adorn false Chicana and Chicano masks are on a non-Chicano Studies intellectual spree. They look and act like Chicanos but curiously they have closed ranks with the former enemies of La Raza—the Elite Intelligentsia. Perhaps the best is yet to come. Whatever, the Chicano Movement has been spared, the fanaticism of the likes of the post-1910 Mexican Revolution infamous anti-cleric socialist fanatic Tomas Garrido Canabal. Garrido Canabal, governor of Tabasco, removed the crosses from gravestones and suppressed the word "adios." On his ranch he had a bull he named God, a donkey named Christ, a cow the *Virgen de Guadalupe,* a hog called the pope. His son was named Lenin and a nephew named Luzbel or Lucifer. Unlike most Chicanos few Mexicans have not heard of Garrido Canabal's "pecados" (sins).

MACHOPHOBIA: *QUE HOMBRE* OR *QUE MACHO?*

Many brown feminists and lesbians, like a majority of white Americans, see a macho in every brown Mexican or Chicano face; and, with that perception a fancied potential sexual predator and pervert. Anti-Mexicanism and misandry are often major factors for those attitudes. Curiously, Mexican men view Mexican Americans as emasculated males, not as machos. Mexico is a patriarchal society shaped from a blend of Spanish and indigenous cultures that were both patriarchal. In more recent history exaggerated masculinity was a serious social problem in Mexico. Two decades of intermittent civil war, the 1910 Revolution and the religious civil war of the 1920s bred brutal behavior among many combatants. The killing ended but the psychological damage remained, particularly the primitive urges turned loose during war. Those impulses are not suddenly withdrawn by all men. That was the social condition in Mexico throughout the 1920s and 1930s. Some became thugs or *pelados.*

Samuel Ramos wrote about the so-called *pelado* in his profile of the Mexican not long after the civil wars as did Octavio Paz in poetry. Later, Oscar Lewis, *Tepoztlan,* and more recently Matthew Gutmann, in *The Meanings of Being Macho,* and others wrote studies regarding exaggerated masculine behavior and machismo in Mexico. Lewis concluded that women admire very masculine men but prefer to marry men who are not too masculine. Their research also concluded that most couples work out their marital roles themselves once they are married. Of course, there are variations of male behavior consistent on whether they are urban or rural, professionals or *rancheros*.

The stereotypical Mexican macho type fancied in the United States humors many Mexicans. In truth many machophobic neo-Chicanas and white women presume too much when their emotions are mired in stereotypical images of sordid lecherous Mexican males. A cursory review of their machophobia reflects much misunderstanding or ignorance of general masculine behavior. Women mistakenly connect erratic behavior in adolescence, which is a marginal period in personality development, with machismo. Boys often try to behave like adults and attempts to prove their masculinity often leads to alcohol, drugs, and sex abuse in concert with violence and vandalism. Adolescent male conduct toward women is not machismo. It may be crude, bold, rash, selfish, and self-centered adolescent behavior but it is not machismo. A central point to understand is that most Chicanos and neo-Chicanos like most white Americans are still adolescents when they enter a college campus culture.

College culture is a sub-culture and frankly another marginal zone wherein young people might experiment with drugs, alcohol, and sex. However, most students discard those social transitory behavioral patterns and leave them behind upon graduating or maturing as they step into the real adult world. During the first years of the Chicano Movement some neo-Chicanas referenced that pattern of brown male behavior as machismo when in actuality it was a clear case of a college adolescent student playing out the campus casanova or sex predator role. Conversely, similar white or black male behavior was not adjudged to be machismo by brown women and others.

The 1970s was influenced by the free love, illicit drugs, gross vulgarity, and alcoholic spectacles of the middle-class hippie counter culture. On and off campus, Americans witnessed some of the most irresponsible behavior imaginable by hippies. Yet, most hippie participants left those irregular social patterns behind upon graduating. In similar manner, some neo-Chicanas emulated their white women co-students by publicly consorting with black male students, too. The neo-Chicanas as mentioned above did not deride black males as vile machos for their masculine behavior. The hippie counter-culture undermined values systems and left vestiges of their counter-culture madness: ear rings, nose rings, penis rings, and belly rings, excessive self-centeredness, less respect for institutional authority, and the male long hair custom. Like most liberal whites and blacks, they did not support the Chicano Movement on campuses. In their view "Chicanos had cultural hang-ups!" Hippies like other whites could not relate to neo-Chicanismo; nor could marginalized neo-Chicanas for the same reasons.

Brown hoodlums, like all hoodlums regardless of race or culture, are unquestionably socially marginal. In this regard brown marginal personalities often behave as adolescents do. They are Don Juanistic, self-centered, immature, and irresponsible. Like many others, neo-Chicanas perceived it as Mexican or Chicano behavior on college campuses and in Movement social interactions because the male perpetrator was a brown man or a Chicano. To the biased perceiver it was expected behavior. And what was particularly absurd was that often the brown male offender might not have even been Spanish-speaking. Was the behavior then presumed to be an inherited character trait or genetic rather than learned? Professor Miguel Montiel affirmed the seriousness of the fallacy of machismo nearly fifty years ago when Chicano scholars were challenging the stereotypical writings of *gabacho* "experts" on Mexican American culture. He wrote, "terms like machismo are abstract, value-laden concepts that lack the empirical referents necessary for construction of sound explanations."[129]

MISANDRY: POVERTY AND MEXICAN FATHERS

In autobiographical sketches many female critics reveal having had difficult experiences with their Mexican fathers. It is an experience which cannot be dismissed as a basis of their machophobia along with with their strong anti-Mexican cultural sentiments. Bear in mind, not their Chicano fathers, but their Mexican fathers. The clash of cultural values systems between Mexican fathers and American-reared daughters can be complex and is the cause of serious psychological disorders. A clear example is Gloria Anzaldua, who although she was a sixth generation Mexican American was reared along the Texas–Mexico border region.

---

129. Montiel, *El Grito,* op. cit.

Her border experiences nurtured many negative sentiments and "indifference to many Mexican cultural values." Most border cultures are commonly lower working class due to the poverty and transitional character of many of its inhabitants. Indeed, southern Texas border life is not particularly contrasting either. Some of the most economically deprived Mexican Americans reside in south Texas towns and cities. Thus, Anzaldua's aversions and personal anxiety was most likely impacted by an ambience of poverty and the lower class behavior of the community in which she lived rather than "Mexican culture" per se; her personal affections also laid elsewhere.

Indeed, Anzaldua's reaction had much deeper personal consequences. First she learned about homosexuality and lesbianism and about feminism from a relationship with her *gabacho* gay friend, Randy Comer, who "really impacted" her life. She always "had an affection for white homosexuals."[130] She asserted that voluntarily she became a lesbian to break the patriarchal system within her own family. In effect, that by so becoming a lesbian she would not have grandchildren that would perpetuate the family line. How true that confession might have been only she would know. She also resented her mother's passive demeanor because it disturbed her more assertive nature.[131] So much for *amor propio* and *cariño* for La Raza. Although she asserts she cared for her father, a certain percentage of Mexican masculine dominant fathers tend to be less flexible and democratic with their maturing daughters. Such social patterns are more common in rural Mexican life then in dysfunctional border town life which is socially transitional.

As discussed in Chapter 4, Mexicans and Chicanos in the United States experience competitive parent modeling. The biological home is in competition with the public school. Biological parents compete with the teachers as role models. The competition presents an experience that adds to stress and anxiety to the already difficult adolescent years. This psychological experience is the root of anti-Mexican sentiments. Although, it should be noted, that is not the case in all homes with Mexican or Chicano parents. However, the argument holds that a Chicano child is influenced and stressed a great deal by the dual parental modeling experience.

---

130. Ann E. Reuman and Gloria Azaldua, *Melus,* Vol. 25. No. 2. Latino/a Identities (Summer, 2000), p. 36.

131. Interview with Gloria Anzaldua, May, 2006.

The very fact that the school's expectations generate gradual and subtle Chicano de-socialization and disenchantment with the biological parents is critical. Those who have studied its negative impact on Chicano children know it well. People refer to it as the melting pot process. In this study we call it "false" Americanism which is the same process. Corky Gonzales captured it well in the poem "I am Joaquin." "I look at myself and see part of me who rejects my father and mother, and dissolves into the melting pot to disappear in shame. And, reclaim my Raza for my own when society gives me token leadership in society's own name." Well-versed and culturally sensitive Chicano scholars concur this discribes the role neo-Chicana intellectualizing intonates in the ivory tower in society's own name.

Some brown women caught in the American Mexican cultural quandary noted above fantasize about being lesbians or choose to be so to escape the self-ascribed wretched role of being a sex object. Anzaldua voluntarily elected to be a lesbian but as revenge against her own father. Thus, it is evident the central conflicting cultural and theological root of the gender problem among the liberated non-Chicanas and lesbians is sexual.[132] And, since sex transcends race, gender, ethnicity, and class, lesbianism is similarly transcultural. Thus, it is a proverbial counter to charge Mexican patriarchy or alleged machismo for the rigid demands for role playing and obedience. Followed in turn by the imbued cultural *santita* role demanded of women by Marianism in Mexican culture; meaning of all things, the Virgen de Guadalupe. Theoretically, in this context women should be chaste, modest, or *santitas* and refrain from becoming sexual objects of every man's imagined lusts. Men are not so restrained. Yet, few Americans are aware of the strength of character of Mexican women and their ability to control their husband's behavior. Moreover, the 1917 Mexican Constitution legally affords women many alternatives to liberate themselves from abusive husbands. Like in the United States, marital decisions are ultimately husband and wife decisions.

The historical record illustrates that no Virgen de Guadalupe was invoked in centuries before the Spanish introduced Christianity and the Virgen de Guadalupe appeared. Yet, Nahua parents admonished their daughters not to follow their hearts, because they would deceive and corrupt themselves, and dishonor their parents. They were also advised

---

132. Hurtado, "Sitios y Lenguas," op. cit.

not to succumb to the public flirtatious intonations of strange men. Chastity, modesty, and good morals were taught the young girls from age five until they married in pre-Columbian central Mexico times.[133] While it is clear that indigenous parental admonishments to be moral in the Valley of Anahuac were comparable to the moral standard introduced by Spanish missionaries, where is the justification to return to pre-Hispanic indigenous values since they were congenial with those introduced by the Spanish?

INDIGENISM IN AZTLAN: EUROAMERICAN STYLE

Many indigenous cultures in Mexico survived the Spanish colonial period, some almost intact with a minimum of cultural diffusion. In Nahua speaking central Mexico the demonic cosmic gods were gone and all traces of the Cult of Huitzilopochtli expressed in the art, architecture, music, dance, and legends eradicated. The culture of war, human sacrifice, and ritual cannibalism sanctioned the old homicidal way as evil regardless of the religious intention. Without war the indigenous nations bonded as the great cultural benefits of Spain's rich culture became self-evident. The indigenous people were preliterate but possessed abstract and creative minds. Thus, learning to read and write their native languages as taught by the friars was a tremendous benefit. With a written language at hand it assisted them in perpetuating and recording the positive major aspects of their cultures during the colonial period. In this vein "during the second half of the sixteenth century a rebirth of native culture took place," wrote George C. Vaillant. "It was encouraged by the Spanish emphasis on hereditary rights to title and property." The evidence of it is found in the writings of indigenous authors like Tezozomoc, Chimalpahin, and others.

The central Mexican peoples fused the acceptable ideas of both cultures. Indigenous culture was not annihilated. Frankly, it was a mutual transcultural process. To this very day the resultant by-product is evidenced in Mexican statuary, sacred music, churches, and ritualistic dancing. So indeed was much of the spiritual aspect of the people retained. One must bear in mind that the people were quite rational and sophisticated. In more recent times secular foreign ideologies have been the cause of civil wars that have caused much death and suffering

---

133. Mendieta, *Historia eclesiastica indiana,* Mexico, D.F: Editorial Porrua, 1971, pp. 119–120.

in Mexico. Despite critical clashes at times the documented colonial past illustrates that the indigenous peoples gained considerably in all aspects of their lives from royal government policies, thanks mostly to the Spanish missionaries.

In the 1960s the Native American anthropologist, Jack D. Forbes, encouraged Mexican Americans to accept their Indianness rather than their presumed Spanishness. Forbes was a precursor of the Chicano Movement. His pre-movement activism earned him the mocking title among cynical professional Mexican Americans at conferences he attended as "the great white father." The surname Forbes, his light skin and his light hair were the characteristics that begot him that absurd label. Most were unaware he was Native American. Mexican Americans at the time were of a different mind-set and thus failed to grasp the pro-indigenous message. Most Mexican Americans were far from wanting to be Indian and were in no mood to compromise their "honorable white" status as they were in the throes of the "false" American process.

The original Mexica Movement of the 1960s promoted a similar philosophy, "pride of Indianness and native to this land in which we preempted the whites." The idea was collective self-identity for political empowerment. Fundamentally, all did not fall on deaf ears. Alurista, a Mexican artist and poet, included indigenous themes in his poetry and Corky Gonzales of Denver, Colorado, enlarged upon the indigenous theme in his poem, "I am Joaquin." The neo-Chicanos were, like their parents, aspiring to be white and to be accepted as full-fledged American. Years of "false" American socialization had fixed their cortical impulses to want to be white. But a few who once having identified themselves as Spanish, *catalanes, espanoles,* and *castellanos,* at first accepted the Mexican American label, then adopted the indigenous barrio identity Chicano. However, the acceptance of the ultimate level of Indian identity was more difficult for most. Among those who accepted the indigenous title it, of course, had to be Aztec Indianness.

However, the neo-Chicano leaders elected to emulate the post-1910 Mexican Revolutionary socialist intellectuals by calling themselves *mestizos.* They adopted the idea from the Mexican and American elite intelligentsias. Emotion won the day as they compromised to use the anti-Indian colonial label for a mythical *mestizo* nation in Aztlan. Thus, they were neither white nor brown but a blend of the two. This decision reaffirmed them as half-breed bastards in the eyes of the *gabacho* intellectuals whose mothers, according to them, were raped by the Spanish conquerors. Unlike black Americans who reject being called mulattos, neo-Chicanos accepted the *mestizo* label for lack of a better available term to fulfill their psychological identity void. Though few neo-Chicanos accepted the indigenous label wholeheartedly, the indigenous notion and desired Indian connection did not end. Chicano artists in the barrios continued to image the swarthy Indian with Chicano identity as before the movement.

CON EL NOPAL AQUI: AND THE WANNABE INDIANS

The neo-Chicana movement in the early 1980s re-resurrected the indigenous past with different intent, but not unlike Mexican socialists who romanticized and resurrected the pre-Columbian past principally to disclaim the Hispanic past and Catholicism. Those neo-Chicanas stranded in "a space between" or a spiritual void sought the "true" pre-Hispanic culture in indigenous identity and Native American spiritualism. Ironically, it was the spiritualism of La Raza, the bond of Hispano-Mexicanism which they had never possessed or had lost in the "false" American process. Like most Americans they had learned in school that the Spanish slaughtered the Indians and the Indians were gone. Richard Rodriguez, author of *Hunger of Memory,* presents us with a more accurate and realistic assessment. He informs us that Spanish is now an Indian language and Christianity is an Indian religion in the Western Hemisphere. "There are more Christians south of the border than in Europe," wrote Rodriguez. "The evangelical Guatemala Indians will come to convert the white Americans some day. The Indian is much alive. They daily cross the border into the United States."[134]

The narration found in some *gabacha* and socialist writings wherein they paint a more idealist indigenous world where women were held in higher esteem in pre-Columbian times attracted many neo-Chicanas and continues to do so. The notion grew in scope and was embellished despite the knowledge or lack of it that a woman was a non-persona caught in a degrading polygamous social condition in pre-colonial Mexico. Polygamy was common throughout indigenous Mexico. Although Nahua women possessed some rights and could be defended in tribunals when necessary, a woman was an object. Some of the so-called "Lords of Nahua" in central Mexico had hundreds of "wives."

---

134. *Los Angeles Times,* Oct. 9, 1992.

Moctezuma had a thousand "wives." Beyond the borders of Aztec civility incest was commonplace among the barbarous nomadic Chichimecos. Also, the Nahua punishment for abortion, incest, adultery, and homosexuality was death. To complain was fruitless because it was a way of life and the Nahua were fatalistic.

In Nahua culture a childbearing woman who died in giving birth merited the highest paradise like a warrior who was vanquished in battle. There were many female slaves. Malinalli, best known as Marina, who was of high Maya birth, was one of nineteen such slaves offered to the Spaniards following their victory over the Tabascos who attacked them. Later, Moctezuma offered one of his many daughters to Cortes. Bandelier wrote that "woman was little better than a costly animal" and "the most degrading epithet which could be addressed to any Mexican, aside from calling him a dog, was that of a woman." Sex and war were the principal motives in Aztec life, and sex activity was religiously motivated. The "love" goddesses of the Aztecs were numerous and they were all associated with horrifying death. However, phallic worship was not found among them although sketchy evidence suggests it was possible among the Maya.

The idol of the blood-thirsty God Huitzilopochtli's mother, Coatlicue, is a grotesque anti-human image as the distinguished novelist Carlos Fuentes once observed. She was the goddess of life and death and was made from human body parts. She was called the "dirt devourer." In total contrast, the Greeks adored the human form as it was chiseled beautifully in stone and marble. A wailing Aztec Goddess who hated men and whose imagined power was disarmed by Spanish missionaries became the harmless La Llorona. A neo-Chicana ivory tower fancy notion to resurrect indigenous spiritualism is based on the mistaken assumption that the Nahua were a humanistic spiritual society. They were spiritual, but like their gods, they were not humanistic.

Nahua psychology was chronicled as passive, meek, and docile although they were great warriors, in particular the nations of central Mexico. Spanish friars appreciated the numerous Catholic values that were congenial with the then-psychology of the central Mexican Nahua. The social position of women was quite specific as any well-versed scholar can relate. The historical record illustrates "most of their chants in relation to the other sex are erotic, not emotional. They responded only to the urges of the 'blood soul'; the 'spirit soul,' speaking by and large did not exist for them."

Frankly speaking, to resurrect and honor the statuary of such dark deities by reciting their ritualistic chants or to follow an imaginary spiritual "Coatlicue state" as was concocted by Anzaldua is literary fantasy. Such whimsy is comparable to satanic worship cults in the United States which is definitely not a society driven by cosmic processes. Moreover, it is most certainly irrelevant to Mexican or Chicano culture that rests on the Catholic foundations that eradicated the Cult of Huitzilopochtli and forged a new fraternity through cultural diffusion that evolved as Mexicanism. Corky Gonzales, who did not possess a college education, called the new cultural bond *carnalismo*. Carnalismo is, in fact, the mainstay of La Raza. That spirit moves his historic poem. And like an oracle Corky enlightens Chicanos that *carnalismo* lost is the major cause for the Mexican American's psychological labyrinth in the secular United States.

Nevertheless, it is remarkable and perhaps lamentable that many Mexican Americans have been so indoctrinated as to look beyond the eradication of war, human sacrifice, and polygamy in the encounter between the Mexica and the Spanish as if those evils had never existed in Mexico. Indeed, with spirited neo-Chicanas or Chicana pretenders resurrecting satanic icons that were the justification for homicide on a grand scale, where is the need to perpetuate the Black Legend wherein Spain's ideological enemies suggest the greatest genocide of the indigenous population occurred?

Richard Rodriguez's words are most appropriate to cap this theme: "The industrial world romanticize the Indian who no longer exist ignoring the Indian who does." Yes, for those who are devoid of perceptual blindness and who may care to look beyond the *gabacho's* veil of ignorance Chicanos and most *Mexicoehuani* (Mexican Americans) are the living Indians among us. Corky cleared the air forever: "Yaqui. Tarahumara, Chamala, Zapotec, . . ." And, he alluded to Apaches and Comanches too. For Chicanos are as native to the land as the nopal, teosinte, and the mesquite and like those plants they have prevailed despite the intrusion of the white Europeans whose tormenting winds have created a painful labyrinth for Chicanos.

Whereas Corky Gonzales recited the resistant chant that Chicanos refused to be absorbed as non-Chicanos in the United States, it was the great Mexican intellectual, Jose Vasconcelos, who mused that Native Americans would one day absorb all the non-indigenous peoples in the Western Hemisphere. In this regard, Chicanos encourage inclusion, they do not promote separatism as some culturally alienated Mexican Americans allege. Chicanos have no rational purpose or need to establish a culture of separation like the United States engineered with its colored skinned minorities following the conquest of Aztlan in 1848.

The Spanish shared their most prized possession, their religion, with the Native Americans, but the Anglo-Americans refused to share their prized institutions of freedom with the Mexicans; whereas, the Mexican Native Americans became Catholics and equal subjects of the Spanish monarchy. Conversely, in the supposedly more progressive republic Mexican Americans were forced to live in barrios as colonized second-class citizens. When Mexican Americans leave the barrio or are reared beyond a barrio culture now, they are mired in a labyrinth of solitude due to the enmity between the *gabacho* individualistic way of life and the Chicano communal way. That, in brief, is the acknowledged new nepantla wherein lies confusion, chaos, and pain, but it offers those caught in the middle time for reflection. In view of the social conditioning examined in this study, introspection about La Raza is generally negative.

Glossary

Amor proprio—literally self-love and self-esteem in one's given culture.

Anglo—defines an American citizen of European descent; it can also mean a person of Mexican, African, or Asian background who has completely adapted to the dominant American culture. Thus, there are brown, black, or Asian Anglos.

Apostate—the abandonment of the Christian faith or religion.

Assimilation—theoretically to make socially and intellectually similar and equal.

Aztlan—the mythical place of origin of the Mexica and other tribal ancient Mexicans. Described as the bright land to the far north. According to most accounts a region inclusive of the United States southwest and California.

Barrio—a district, section, or neighborhood of a larger community. Normally a counter-cultural impoverished social enclave with a history composed of Spanish surnamed, bilingual, bicultural brown-skinned persons generally assumed to be "Mexican" by most Americans. Its modern origins are post-1848 when the United States conquered the Southwest and California from Mexico and established a Culture of Separation (term coined by author) for Mexicans, Native Americans (reservations), and Chinese Chinatowns and after the Civil War, ghettos for black Americans. Literally spaces in-between white Americans and colored Americans.

B.A.S.P.—literally, brown Anglo-Saxon and (republican) Protestant. A brown counterpart to the W.A.S.P. notion of what constitutes an ideal American in the "False" American sense. (Term coined by the author.)

B.A.S.P. Aspirant—a Mexican American of Chicano or Mexican origin who is in cultural transition or socially marginalized, a nepantla stage. This aspiration suspends the person between his host culture and a sought after "full-fledged Americanism." (Term coined by the author.)

Beaner—a disparaging reference in pre-Chicano Movement years made by white American adolescents of Mexican American youths in the Southwest.

Carnalismo—biological and cultural fraternity founded on Catholic precepts of universal humanity. Hermandad in Spanish and brotherhood in English.

Castanoid—the reddish-brown or castaño Native American population, including Mexicans and Chicanos who are of part or unmixed indigenous ancestry. (Term coined by the author.)

Chicanismo—the by-product of both the de-socialization and Americanization processes encountered by Mexican Americans principally since the last world war. Urbanization has also contributed to the emergence of Chicanismo. It is a bilingual, bicultural insulated counter culture bred by the forced imposition of a Culture of Separation.

Chicano—abbreviation for Mexica (Meschica). The term evolved as a Spanish colonial practice of abbreviating the indigenous peoples of Mexico. Thus, indios Chicanos were distinguished from indios mecos (Chichimecos) and other tribes or nations in this manner. In the United States the appellation has acquired two distinctive definitions. First, it identifies a Mexican American active in the Chicano Movement, and second, it more accurately describes a Mexican American born and reared in a counter-cultural barrio.

Chicanos/as falsos/as—persons of Mexican descent born in the United States who, although not in cultural harmony with counter-cultural barrio Chicanos or the tenets of the Chicano Movement of self-determination, self-ascribe the label for self-aggrandizement.

Chicano Movement—generally a B.A.S.P. Aspirant inspired cultural nationalist movement and crusade against the mono-cultural credos of "False" Americanism. Goals were self-determination and the mandate to be accorded equality in all aspects of American life like other Americans.

Chichimecas—(Nahuatl) barbarians, wild tribes located in northern pre-Columbian Mexico.

Cholos/as—a low caste Mexican national type to Mexican Americans. In the Southwest the term also applies to street young people, both genders, who belong to gangs and exhibit certain anti-social behavioral patterns. A barrio sub-culture.

Chuntaros—at point of Spanish contact the root word chuntal meant a barbarian or referred to a person who was not too bright. The term is applied to Mexican nationals and mentally slow gang members by Chicano street youths who belong to gangs and exhibit certain anti-social behavioral patterns.

Counter-cultural—an ongoing encounter between Mexicanism and "false" Americanism, and since World War II, between Chicanismo and "false" Americanism in the former Mexican provinces.

Creole—in colonial New Spain (Mexico), persons of Spanish "blood" born in the colony. A culturally suspended minority of New Spain in colonial times and the post-Mexican Revolution period.

Deculturate—a socio-psychological de-socialization process by which a person is disinherited usually through the schools without reciprocal compensation.

De-socialization—stripping a person of his host cultural values and identity.

Elitist—in this study the Ivory tower's presumptuous canons or postulations; superior attitudes.

"False" Americanism—republican Protestantism, Christo-republicanism; those elements of the American Way of life which took on a "religious-like" stature due to the enshrouding of the secular humanist religio-philosophical credos of the country with a biblical and Christian language and symbolism. In brief, the so-called melting pot notion.

Gabacho—this term is Spanish in origin. During the Napoleonic era Spaniards in the Pyrenees who sided with the French were considered traitors and called gabachos. Among Chicanos in the barrios of the Southwest, it refers to an Anglo person who is culturally a non-Chicano.

Hispano—a title held by many persons in New Mexico who claim Spanish lineage from the first Spanish family settlers in 1598.

Internal colonialism—a Culture of Separation situation or condition wherein a colored or ethnic minority is forced to acquiesce to a political, economic, and social powerless existence.

La Raza—a term used to identify the corporate personality or spiritual cohesion of the Hispano-Castaño people of the Americas. El Dia de La Raza celebrated in Mexico and in South America commemorating the coming together of two peoples—the Spanish and the Native Americans. It is Columbus Day in the United States.

Machiotl—referenced as an all-around Aztec warrior in pre-Hispanic Mexica culture. Brave in battle, versed in the mythological religion, cultured, loyal, and a responsible man.

Machismo—two definitions are applicable in Mexico. First, among the better classes it suggests positive and acceptable male characteristics with a modicum of social etiquette. Second, among the lower classes the term generally connotes negative and exaggerated male attributes of a physical character. In Anglo-American popular culture the second category has found widespread acceptance as a term to demean and denounce unacceptable masculine behavior. Transitional adolescent or adult marginal behavior is not machismo. Youngsters are maturing in the first case, and in the second case it is neurotic behavior.

Melting pot—a secular humanist notion of universalism, "false" American. In brief, it is a form of rejection of a person's natural right "to be" as an American guaranteed by the Constitution.

Mestizaje—a pejorative term connected with Spanish colonialism to socially control the progeny of mixed-bloods. Normally in reference to a white and Indian half-breed.

Mestizo—a disparaging anti-Indian colonial term used to describe a half-breed cross between an "Indian" and a European. However, a mestizo was still an Indian by blood.

Mexican—the word stemmed from Mexica. In 1821 the creole insurgents adopted the term to name the new nation which included all persons born in Mexico including themselves. In correct usage it means a Mexican national. It is not a race label.

Mexicoehuani—a Mexican American in Nahua. Term coined by Mario E. Aguilar.

Nativism—an exclusive native "false" American doctrine, i.e., American for white Americans only.

Neo-Chicana feminism—whereas equality for Mexican American women is the aim, it also promotes an ideology based on rejection of Chicanismo and traditional cultural values regarding masculinity, femininity, and religion. The proponents of neo-Chicana feminism include neo-Chicanas and Chicanas falsas who promote an ideology that is similar to the mainstream Women's Liberation movement with secular principles on gender roles and sexuality.

Neo-Chicanas—Mexican American women who shaped their own literary and political movement expanding their porous framework of analysis beyond race and ethnicity. Despite their non-Chicano focus they allege to be Chicanas.

Neo-Chicanismo—the religio-philosophical ideology of B.A.S.P. Aspirants and Chicanos who gave birth to a political form of Chicanismo; an active brown American counter-cultural ethos of Anglo-American society.

Neo-Chicano—a B.A.S.P. Aspirant who converts to neo-Chicanismo and is in concert with the Movement's self-determination political goals. (Term coined by the author.)

Nepantla—the nahua word of "space between" which was enlarged and incorporated in Gloria Anzaldua's literary theories.

Patas rajadas—a disparaging term used by Mexican Americans between 1910 and 1970 in reference to Mexican peon immigrants. Literally the term means scarred feet.

Pingo—demon, evil spirit (Nahuatl). The Aztecs offered human hearts in accordance with their calendar of pingos. In modern usage it describes naughty behavior.

Plan de Aztlan—the philosophy and creed of cultural nationalism; for self-determination for the people of Aztlan. Expressing the right of Mexican Americans to be accepted as Chicanos.

Pocho—literally a faded Mexican. A demeaning term used by Mexicans to describe Mexican Americans generally. It suggests cultural and racial alienation.

Proselytism—the act of being a proselyte against Catholicism and for Protestantism.

Puto—a label used by Chicanos active in the Chicano Movement to expose and purge co-opted vendidos who could not be trusted; prostitutes or whores.

Syncretism—an untenable compromise between Christian beliefs and secular or pagan beliefs.

Teosinte—the wild Mexico plant (maize) hybridized by pre-Columbian Native Americans in the Valley of Anahuac. DNA has proved it is native to Mexico.

Texas Game—the so-called tactic applied in conquering Texas by encouraging a large immigration of Americans to enter the province and become Mexican citizens, thereby outnumbering the native Mexicans and in time wresting control of the area from Mexico with American filibusters and United States government support.

Tribal Mexico—that part of north central Mexico which lay beyond the boundaries of the civilized central valley nations.

"True" Americanism—birthright, citizenship, participation in the democratic and republican institution processes, protected by the Constitution, the Bill of Rights, political equality, participation in the process of freedom, and the formal structure of civil authority.

Vendido/a—a person of Mexican descent who is an opportunist. A vendido/a uses his or her ethnic and racial extraction for self-aggrandizement. Such a person is what has variously been described in the past as a professional Mexican by the Anglo community and a coyote by the Mexicans.

Wetback—a casual term used among Mexican Americans in reference to a Mexican national.

CHAPTER 1
The Formative Years: Self-Images and Expectations

Key Terms

egocentric level	mental block
normal behavior	reference group
sense rejection	ego strength
alternative concepts	macho fathers
three "r's"	self-esteem

Discussion Questions

1. According to educators what constitutes Americanization?

2. How does bilingualism affect Americanization?

3. A Chicano child's sense of rejection means what? Explain.

4. What does verbalism mean to educators?

5. Discuss the effect of television on Chicano children.

6. What is meant by a social curriculum in education?

CHAPTER 2
The Formative Years: Desocialization and Alienation

Key Terms

core curriculum   nativism
"Mexican" schools   counter-cultural
barrio life   monosyllabic

Discussion Questions

1. Identify the core curriculum of American education.

2. Is the English language vital to Americanization? How?

3. Explain the difference between social custom and nativism.

4. Do the public schools accommodate barrio children's cultural point of reference? How or why not?

CHAPTER 3
Mexican Stereotypes: A Basis of Hostility

Key Terms

Black Legend   Eurocentric
"Mexican ways"   role-playing
Bato Loco   melting pot

Discussion Questions

1. What are some major elements of American monoculturalism?

2. What is desocialization in the Chicano sense?

3. Is social deviancy innate in Chicano culture?

4. How is differential socialization unfair to Chicanos?

5. What is wrong with Mexican stereotypes?

CHAPTER 4
The Early Adolescent Years: Self-Images and Expectations

Key Terms

capitalist work ethic	success models
"white washed"	Hispanic label
in loco parentis	cultural conflict
authority model	sit-in

Discussion Questions

1. What is meant by academic socialization?

2. Chicanos are not Hispanics. The label does not fit. Why?

3. Why is *"in loco parentis"* critical in Chicano education?

4. What is meant by cultural transition in American society?

5. Can educators be trained to recognize cultural conflict?

6. What constitutes a "potential dropout"?

CHAPTER 5
The Middle School: A Chicano Crossroads

Key Terms

biosocial stage   American ideal
middle school values   inertia
"to make it"   Anglo-like

Discussion Questions

1. What is expected academically in middle school?

2. Why does ethnicity become central in the middle school years?

3. What is withdrawal behavior?

4. "To make it" in American society means what for Chicanos?

5. Are *gente decente* values similar to American middle class values?

6. What impact does United States history have on middle school Chicano children?

CHAPTER 6

Early Adolescent Years: Brown American Authority Models

Key Terms

assimilation	culture of denial
deculturate	ethnocentric
the WASP principal	"beaner"
social recognition	egalitarian
"paddies"	*"gabachos"*

Discussion Questions

1. What is meant by psychological apartheid?

2. Why do Chicanos see American society as Eurocentric?

3. Is the social curriculum of the public schools monocultural?

4. How does the process of deculturation work?

CHAPTER 7
The Later Adolescent Years: Beyond the Crossroads

Key Terms

biological identity   social exclusion
proselytizer   gang culture
Pachuco   "being somebody"

Discussion Questions

1. Does American culture possess anti-Mexican sentiments that affect the educational process of Chicano children?

2. Has a definitive educational pattern been established for the education of "Mexicans" in American public schools?

3. Why were Mexicans denied an equal educational opportunity in the past?

4. Are hostile barrio gangs a by-product of public school policies?

5. If being a "Mexican" in American society is a nobody, how can a Chicano ever become somebody?

6. How is the loss of self-esteem by Chicano youngsters significant in their education?

CHAPTER 8
The Timeless Philosophical Impasse: Nature vs. God

Key Terms

Catholic culture   subjectivism
Agnosticism   "false" Americanism
corporate personality   conformity

Discussion Questions

1. Why is the English language considered so important as a requirement for Chicanos to be accepted as American?

2. What did regeneration of the Aztlan really mean to the westward bound Americans?

3. Why is American culture's secularism hostile to dogmatic religion such as Catholicism?

4. Jaime Escalante's success among Chicano students is attributable to what?

5. What is meant by a cultural gap?

CHAPTER 9
Later Adolescence and the Dark Side of Ethnocide:
The *Bato Loco* Fantasy

Key Terms

generation gap   emasculated
ethnic oppression   child abuse
pathological behavior   *bato loco* fantasy

Discussion Questions

1. How can Chicano student modes of behavior be properly assessed?

2. Does the generation gap also affect Chicano students?

3. What are some counter-cultural American values that clash with Chicano ones?

4. How can child abuse be defined in the Chicano educational experience?

5. Do the schools nurture pathological behavior among Chicano students?

6. How does brown race denial contribute toward hostile gang activity?

7. Is athletics useful for developing character among Chicano students?

CHAPTER 10
A Deplorable School Record: Barriers to Being Somebody

Key Terms

operant conditioning
pseudo-learning
Marxist socialism
neo-Chicano

spoon-feeding
formative years
social ostracism
"to be somebody"

Discussion Questions

1. How do the schools generate and effect behavior shaping?

2. In contrast to Chicanos why are white students not separated from their culture?

3. Why do Chicano scholars believe the public school agenda is an emasculator experience for Chicano youngsters?

4. How divisive was Marxist socialist thought during the Chicano movement?

CHAPTER 11
The Internal Colony Labyrinth:
Perpetuating the Consciousness of Inferiority

Key Terms

ethnic bonds   *agabachados*
self-actualization   apartheid policy
ballot-box power   MALDEF

Discussion Questions

1. What are some of the major psychological effects of the schools on students generally?

2. Why are so many Chicanos so-called academic late-bloomers?

3. When does a sense of self-confidence in ethnic and racial awareness occur?

4. Can political power make a significant difference for the Chicano community?

5. How does marginalism affect the Chicano character?

6. What is the long-term effect on the Chicano community of the large dropout rate of Chicano students?

CHAPTER 12
The Internal Colony Labyrinth:
Non-Colonized, Non-Chicano Roles

Key Terms

indios del sur   *indios del norte*
Mayflower   *agringados*
Cristero Rebellion   Alamo

Discussion Questions

1. Why must Chicanos acquiesce to the white supremacists?

2. In what way is American monocultural freedom limiting?

3. What predisposes Mexican Americans to be unfriendly toward Mexican immigrants?

4. How does Lee Trevino's public commentary bolster the majority society's view of "Mexicans"?

5. What is the commonality between the *indios del sur* and the *indios del norte?*

CHAPTER 13
Those Mexicans: A Republican Protestant View

Key Terms

Edward R. Roybal   La Raza
Social Darwinists   Latinos
Aztlan   second-class citizens

Discussion Questions

1. How has the Hispano-Mexican been anathematized in American literature?

2. Do all American schoolchildren learn institutionally acceptable prejudice and biases in school?

3. How had the press stereotyped "Mexicans" and Chicanos?

4. Why is Chicanismo the best of two cultures?

5. How can Chicanos prove they are treated like second-class citizens?

CHAPTER 14
Chicano Nationalism: A New Birth Of Freedom

Key Terms

social movement
neo-Chicano convert
The Establishment

Nazi Germany
Viva La Raza
Law of Nature

Discussion Questions

1. What immediate causes contributed to the emergence of the Chicano ethnic movement?

2. What changes occurred in the Mexican American community following the Second World War?

3. What was the phenomenon of Mexican-Americanization between 1945–1965?

4. How many typologies surfaced within the Mexican American community by the 1960s?

5. Why did the Establishment refuse to accept Chicanismo as an American phenomenon?

CHAPTER 15
Freedom Maligned: The Pathways of "False" Americanism

Discussion Questions

1. What was the focus of the brown feminist movement?

2. Define gendercentric and how it applies to the Chicano experience.

3. What was the focus of the 1971 Chicano Conference at Houston, Texas?

4. How has the Brown Ivory Tower contributed to an anti-cultural nationalist stance in academia?

5. What did the National Organization of Women (N.O.W.) contribute to Neo-Chicana thought?

CHAPTER 16
Anything but Chicano Thought

Discussion Questions

1. How is socialism antithetical to Chicano communalism?

2. What is machophobia and how does it relate to Neo-Chicanas?

3. What is at the root of anti-clericalism among Neo-Chicanas/os?

4. Define "Chicana falsa" and which typology it best represents and why?

5. Compare Chicano Movement era indigenismo with the indigenist spirituality promoted today?

6. What is the connection of brown feminism to postcolonialism?

Index

Author Biography

Dr. E.C. Orozco was born and reared in a southern California barrio. He is the fifth child of a family of ten children born to Agapito Orozco Miramontes of Temastian, Jalisco, Mexico, and Cruz Cardoza Barbalena of Barstow, California. He is a product of Van Nuys High School and California State University at Northridge where he earned his Bachelor of Arts degree. Dr. Orozco was encouraged by the distinguished Native American anthropologist, Jack D. Forbes, to pursue doctoral studies at the University of Southern California. The renowned historian, Manuel P. Servin, served as his mentor at the University of Southern California where he earned his doctorate. Professor Orozco has taught at numerous California colleges and universities including California State Universities at Dominguez Hills, Los Angeles, and Northridge. He has also taught at Woodbury University, Mt. St. Mary's College, and at the University of Guadalajara, Mexico. Dr. Orozco is presently the coordinator of Chicano Studies at Pasadena City College.

The author did post-doctoral work in philosophy and theology at Fuller Theological Seminary in Pasadena, California, and at Los Angeles Valley College in Jewish Studies under the erudite Zev Garber. Professor Orozco authored an intellectual history of the Chicano experience with the title, **Republican Protestantism in Aztlan: The Encounter Between Mexicanism and Anglo-American Secular Humanism in The United States Southwest.** Professor Orozco has an innovative book on race and the Chicano forthcoming in the Fall 2013.